PHOTOSHOP

ert Shufflebotham

OMPUTER
EP

In easy steps is an imprint of Computer Step
Southfield Road . Southam
Warwickshire CV33 OFB . England

Tel: 01926 817999 Fax: 01926 817005
http://www.computerstep.com

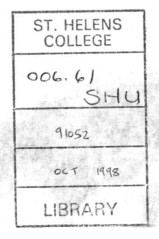
Notice of Liability
Every effort has been made to ensure that this book contains accurate
and current information. However, Computer Step and the author
shall not be liable for any loss or damage suffered by readers as a
result of any information contained herein.

Trademarks
Photoshop, Adobe Illustrator, Pagemaker, and PostScript are
trademarks of Adobe Systems Incorporated. All other trademarks are
acknowledged as belonging to their respective companies.

Printed and bound in the United Kingdom

ISBN 1-874029-82-2

Contents

Basic Theory

Chapter One

An understanding of the basics of colour is important if you are to get the best out of Photoshop. Refer back to this section from time to time. As your understanding of Photoshop grows, so will your appreciation of the concepts of colour that underpin the whole process of image capture and image manipulation.

This section also covers monitor setup and calibration.

Covers

Bitmaps and Vectors

Photoshop is an image-editing application with a wealth of tools and commands for working on digital images or bitmaps. There are utilities for retouching, colour correcting, compositing and more. There are also over 90 functional and creative filters that can be applied to entire images, or selected areas within images.

A bitmap image consists of a rectangular grid, or raster, of pixels – in concept, very much like a mosaic. When you edit a bitmap you are editing the colour values of individual pixels or groups of pixels.

Image-editing applications differ fundamentally from vector-based applications such as Adobe Illustrator and Macromedia FreeHand. In these applications, you work with objects that can be moved, scaled, transformed, stacked and deleted as individual or grouped objects, but all the time each exists as a complete, separate object.

These applications are called vector drawing packages, as each object is defined by a mathematical formula. Because of this, they are resolution-independent – you can scale vector drawings up or down (either in the originating application or in a page layout application such as QuarkXPress or Adobe PageMaker) and they will still print smoothly and crisply.

You should always try to scan an image at, or slightly larger than, the size at which you intend to use it. This means you will avoid having to increase the size of the image.

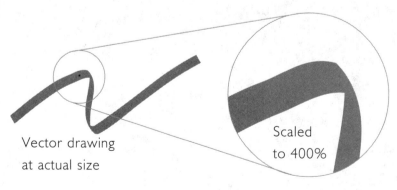

Vector drawing
at actual size

Scaled
to 400%

In contrast, bitmaps are created at a set resolution – a fixed number of pixels per inch. If you scan an image at a specific resolution, then double its size, you are effectively halving its resolution (unless you add more pixels). You are likely to end up with a blocky, jagged image, as you have increased the size of the individual pixels that make up the bitmap image.

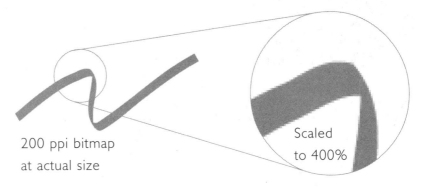

200 ppi bitmap
at actual size

Scaled
to 400%

Bitmaps and Bit-depth

An important factor when the digital data for an image is captured, typically at the scanning stage, is its bit-depth. Bit-depth refers to the amount of digital storage space used to record information about the colour of a pixel. The more bits you use, the more colour information you can store to describe the colour of a pixel – but also, the larger file size you end up with.

REMEMBER

More, rather than less, colour information is usually desirable, as this means the image can represent more shades of colour, with finer transitions between colours and greater density of colour, leading to a more realistic image.

To output realistic images using PostScript technology an image should be able to represent 256 grey levels. A 24-bit scan is sufficient for recording 256 grey levels for each of the Red, Green and Blue channels, resulting in a possible combination of over 16 million colours.

Ideally, when you work on images in Photoshop you will do so using a 24-bit monitor capable of displaying over 16 million colours. This ensures that you see all the colour detail in the image. Although you can work on images using only thousands of colours, for best results, especially where colour reproduction is important, you need to work with as many colours as possible.

Pixels and Resolution

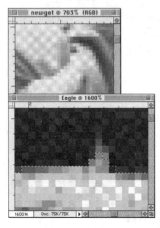

Pixels

A pixel is the smallest element in a bitmap image such as a scan. Pixel is short for 'picture element'. Zoom in on an image in Photoshop and you will start to see the individual pixels – the fundamental building blocks – that make up the image. When working in Photoshop, you are editing pixels, changing their colour, shade and brightness.

Resolution

A key factor when working on bitmap images is resolution. This is measured in pixels per inch (ppi).

Pixels can vary in size. If you have an image with a resolution of 100 ppi, each pixel would be 1/100th of an inch square. In an image with a resolution of 300 ppi, each pixel would be 1/300th of an inch square – giving a much finer, less blocky result.

Printer resolution measured in dots per inch (dpi) is not the same as image resolution measured in pixels per inch (ppi). Printer dots are a fixed size, pixels can vary in size.

When working on images that will eventually be printed on a printing press, you need to work on high-resolution images. These are scanned images whose resolution is twice the halftone screen frequency (measured in lines per inch – lpi) that will be used for final output – that is when you output to bromide or film.

For example, for a final output screen frequency of 150 lpi – a typical screen frequency used for glossy magazines – you need to scan your image at a resolution of 300 ppi.

Resolutions of double the screen frequency are important for images with fine lines, repeating patterns or textures. You can achieve acceptable results, especially when printing at screen frequencies greater than 133 lpi, using resolutions of 1½ times the final screen frequency.

Images intended for multimedia presentations or the World Wide Web need only be 72 ppi, which is effectively the screen resolution.

To work with images for positional purposes only, as long as you can get accurate enough on-screen results and laser proofs, you can work with much lower resolutions.

RGB and CMYK Colour Models

As you start working with Adobe Photoshop there are two colour models that you need to be aware of. These are the RGB (Red, Green, Blue) and CMYK (Cyan, Magenta, Yellow and Black) colour models.

RGB is important because it mirrors the way the human eye perceives colour. It is typically the model used by scanners and digital cameras to capture colour information in digital format, and it is the way that your computer monitor describes colour.

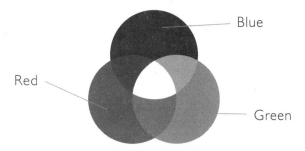

Red, green and blue are referred to as the **additive primaries**. You can add varying proportions of the three colours to produce millions of different colours – but still a more limited range (or 'gamut') than in nature, due to the limitations of the phosphor screen coating of the monitor. If you add 100% red, green and blue light together, you get white. You produce the **secondary** colours when you add red and blue to get magenta; green and blue to get cyan; red and green to get yellow.

The CMYK colour model is referred to as the **subtractive** colour model. It is important because this is the colour model used by printing presses.

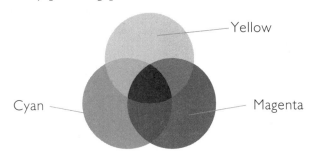

If you subtract all cyan, magenta and yellow when printing you end up with the complete absence of colour – white.

On the printing press, cyan, magenta, yellow and black are combined to simulate a huge variety of colours. Printers add black because, although in theory, if you combine 100% each of cyan, magenta and yellow you produce black, in reality, because of impurities in the dyes, you only get a muddy brown.

Colour Gamuts

Colour gamut refers to the range of colours that a specific device is capable of producing. There are millions of colours in the visible spectrum that the eye can discern. Scanners, monitors and printing presses cannot reproduce every colour in the visible spectrum – the range of colours they are capable of producing is their gamut.

From the desktop publishing point of view, the process of capturing digital colour information, viewing and manipulating this on-screen and then finally printing the image using coloured inks is complicated, because the gamut of a colour monitor is different to the gamut of CMYK and Pantone inks.

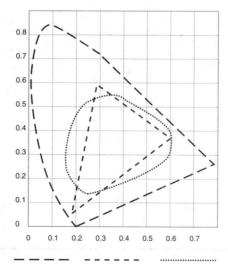

Visible Spectrum   Monitor   SWOP-CMYK

There are colours (especially vibrant yellows and deep blues) that can be displayed on a monitor but cannot be printed using traditional CMYK inks.

Typically, when you work in Photoshop, you will work in RGB (Red, Green, Blue) mode. RGB mode is faster to work in than CMYK mode, and in RGB mode all Photoshop options and commands are available to you. When you have finished making necessary adjustments and corrections to the image, you will need to convert it to CMYK mode, before saving/exporting the image in EPS or TIFF format for use in a page layout application such as Adobe PageMaker or QuarkXPress.

When you convert from RGB to CMYK mode, Photoshop converts out-of-gamut colours (in this case, colours that can be seen on screen, but not printed) into their nearest printable equivalent.

Monitor Calibration (Mac)

BEWARE

If your monitor has its own colour calibration utility, you can use that, or Photoshop's Gamma control panel, but you should not use both.

Follow these steps to adjust your monitor greys so that they are as neutral as possible.

1 Install the Gamma control panel that ships with Photoshop. You can find it in the Photoshop > Goodies > Calibration folder. Drag the Gamma icon into the Control Panels folder in the System Folder. Double-click the icon, then click the On button. Restart your Mac.

2 Change your monitor background to the plain grey default background. This is important for setting a neutral grey, as it prevents interference from other colours or patterns.

HANDY TIP

Make sure that your monitor has warmed up for at least 30 minutes before you set the Gamma controls.

3 Launch Photoshop.

4 Re-open the Gamma control panel. Click a Target Gamma. Use 1.8 for images that will be printed. For images intended for use on the World Wide Web, or in Multimedia presentations, select a Target Gamma of 2.2.

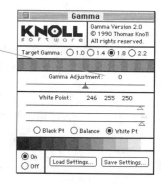

HANDY TIP

You should try to maintain standard lighting conditions in the room you work in to ensure consistent, predictable viewing conditions.

5 Return to Photoshop. Choose File > New. Make sure White is selected for Contents. OK the dialogue box. Make sure you can see the Photoshop window and the Gamma windows.

...contd

6 Click the White Pt button, then hold up a piece of the paper stock on which the image will be printed next to the white background in the Photoshop

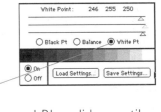

image window. Drag the Red, Green and Blue sliders until the white of the paper matches the background as closely as possible. This is to eliminate any bluish or reddish colour cast.

Use the Save and Load buttons to set up Gamma settings for different lighting conditions at different times of the day and for different paper stocks. (See page 30, Chapter Two for using Save and Load settings options.)

7 Drag the Gamma Adjustment slider until the solid grey bars and the patterned bars match each other as closely as possible.

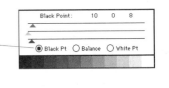

8 Click the Balance button. Look at the grey boxes below Balance. Adjust the sliders to achieve neutral greys with no colour cast.

9 Click Black Pt. Look at the darkest boxes in the strip below Black Pt. Again, adjust the sliders to eliminate any colour cast in the shadow areas.

10 You may need to go back and readjust Balance and Gamma Adjustment. Close the Gamma control panel.

Monitor Calibration (Windows)

BEWARE

If your monitor has its own colour calibration utility, you can use that, or Photoshop's Gamma control panel, but you should not use both.

Monitor calibration is slightly different in the Windows environment.

1 Launch Photoshop. Choose File > New. Make sure White is selected for Contents. OK the dialogue box.

2 Choose File > Colour Settings > Monitor Setup.

3 Enter a target gamma of 1.8 if the image is to be printed. Set a target gamma of 2.2 if the image is intended for multimedia or the World Wide Web. If you make a change to the gamma setting, OK the dialogue box, then reopen it.

HANDY TIP

Make sure that your monitor has warmed up for at least 30 minutes before you set the Gamma controls.

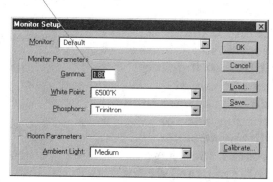

4 Click the Calibrate button. Click the White Pt button, then hold up a piece of the paper stock on which the image will be printed next to the white background in the Photoshop image window. Drag the Red, Green and Blue sliders until the white of the paper matches the background as closely as possible. This is to eliminate any bluish or reddish colour cast.

HANDY TIP

You should try to maintain standard lighting conditions in the room you work in to ensure consistent, predictable viewing conditions.

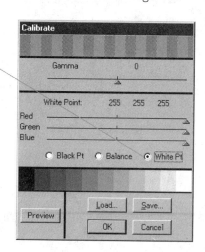

...contd

5 Drag the Gamma Adjustment slider until the solid grey bars and the patterned bars match each other as closely as possible.

6 Click the Balance button. Look at the grey boxes below Balance. Adjust the sliders to achieve neutral greys with no colour cast.

HANDY TIP

Use the Save and Load buttons to set up Gamma settings for different lighting conditions at different times of the day and for different paper stocks. (See page 30 in Chapter Two for using Save and Load settings options.)

7 Click Black Pt. Look at the darkest boxes in the strip below Black Pt. Again, adjust the sliders to eliminate any colour cast in the shadow areas.

8 You may need to go back and readjust Balance and Gamma Adjustment. OK the Gamma control panel and OK the Monitor Setup dialogue box.

Calibrate

Gamma   0

Color Balance: 0   0   0
Red
Green
Blue

○ Black Pt   ⊙ Balance   ○ White Pt

Preview   Load...   Save...
           OK   Cancel

Monitor Setup

Monitor Setup is important because the settings are taken into account when you convert images from one colour mode to another.

 You must do Monitor Setup before you convert an RGB image to CMYK mode. Images already converted to CMYK mode will not be affected by subsequent changes in the Monitor Setup dialogue box.

1 To set up your monitor, choose File > Colour Settings > Monitor Setup.

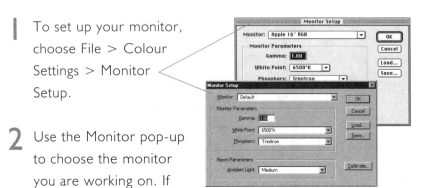

2 Use the Monitor pop-up to choose the monitor you are working on. If your monitor is not listed, choose Default. In Windows, choosing a monitor sets the White Point and Phosphors options automatically.

3 *Macintosh:* Select the same target gamma as you selected in the Gamma setup control panel.
Windows: You will already have entered an appropriate value during the monitor calibration stage (see 'Monitor Calibration (Windows)' on page 16).

4 Use the White Point pop-up to set the value required by any third-party monitor-calibration software. Leave the value at 6500K if you do not need to enter a different value.

5 Use the Ambient Light pop-up to indicate the lighting conditions in the room you are working in. Select High if the room lighting conditions are brighter than the image on your screen; medium if the room and monitor light are roughly equal; low if the screen is brighter than the room lighting.

The Working Environment

This section covers the basics of the Photoshop working environment, getting you used to the Photoshop window, the toolbox, palettes and a number of standard Photoshop conventions that you will find useful as you develop your Photoshop skills.

Chapter Two

Covers

The Photoshop Screen Environment

There are three 'screen modes' to choose from when working on images in Photoshop. The screen mode icons are located at the bottom of the toolbox. Full screen with menu bar mode is useful because it clears away the clutter of the Finder environment on the Mac. Use Full screen mode to see the image without the distraction of other screen elements, and without any other colours interfering with the colours in your image.

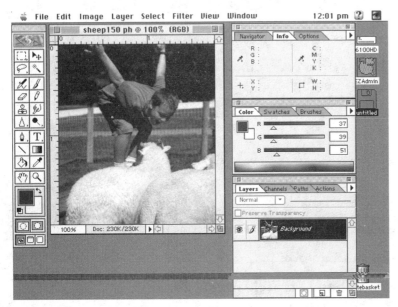

Standard screen mode

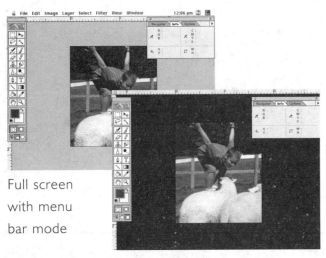

Full screen
with menu
bar mode

Full screen mode

Click this icon to return to Standard screen mode.

2 Click this icon to go to Full screen with menu bar mode.

3 Click this icon to go to Full screen mode. Press the Tab key to hide/show the toolbox and palettes.

...contd

Windows Environment

The Windows environment offers identical functionality to the Macintosh environment, as you can see from a comparison of the Windows and Macintosh screen shots.

The Image Window

HANDY TIP **You need the rulers showing to create ruler guides. Use the shortcut Command/Ctrl + R to show or hide rulers.**

Title bar

Close box

Image

Rulers

Sizes bar

Scroll bars

View Percentage

Resize box

Using the Toolbox

There are a number of useful general techniques that relate to choosing tools in the toolbox.

REMEMBER

The toolbox buttons labelled with italics on the right can be used to access a whole group of related tools, which are shown under 'Hidden Tools'. See steps 2 and 3 on the following page.

Marquee (M)	Move (V)
Lasso (L)	Magic wand (W)
Airbrush (A)	Paintbrush (B)
Eraser (E)	Pencil (Y)
Rubber stamp (S)	Smudge (U)
Blur (R)	*Dodge (O)*
Pen (P)	*Type (T)*
Line (N)	Gradient (G)
Paint bucket (K)	Eyedropper (I)
Hand (H)	Zoom (Z)
Foreground colour	Switch colours (X)
Default colours (D)	Background colour
Standard mode (Q)	Quick Mask mode (Q)
Standard screen mode (F)	Full screen mode (F)

Hidden Tools

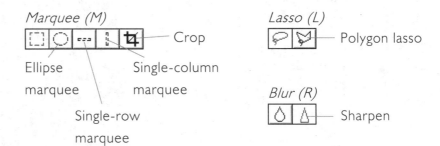

Marquee (M) — Crop

Ellipse marquee

Single-column marquee

Single-row marquee

Lasso (L) — Polygon lasso

Blur (R) — Sharpen

...contd

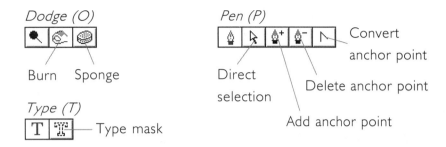

Dodge (O)

Burn   Sponge

Type (T)

T 𝕋 —— Type mask

Pen (P)

Convert anchor point

Direct selection

Delete anchor point

Add anchor point

1 Press the keyboard shortcut to access tools quickly and easily.

2 Click and hold on any tool with a small triangle in the bottom right corner to see all tools in that tool group.

3 Hold down Alt/Option (Mac), or Alt (Windows) and click on any tool in a tool group to cycle through the available tools. Alternatively, press the keyboard shortcut for that tool group a number of times. For example, press 'O' three times to cycle through all the tools in the Dodge tool group.

4 Press Tab to hide/show all palettes, including the toolbox.

5 Double-click on a tool to show the appropriate Options palette for that tool.

HANDY TIP

Use Display & Cursor Preferences in the File menu to change the default appearance of painting and other Cursors.

6 Press Caps Lock to change painting cursors to a precise crosshair cursor, which indicates the centre of the painting tool. Press Caps Lock again to return to standard cursors.

Document and Scratch Sizes

The Sizes Bar is useful for monitoring disk space and memory considerations as you work on your images.

Document Sizes

With Document Sizes selected, you will see two numbers separated by a slash. The first number is the size of the image when all layers are flattened. The second number may be larger and represents the file storage size, whilst the image contains additional layers you may have set up. In images that consist of only a single layer, both numbers are the same.

Scratch Sizes

The Scratch disk is an underlying technical detail that you should be aware of when using Photoshop. The Scratch disk is a designated hard disk that Photoshop utilises as 'virtual' memory if it runs out of memory (RAM) whilst working on one or more images.

With Scratch Sizes selected in the Sizes Bar you again see two numbers separated by a slash. The first number represents the amount of memory (RAM) Photoshop needs to handle all currently open pictures. The second number represents the actual amount of memory available to Photoshop. When the first number is greater than the second, Photoshop is using the Scratch disk as virtual memory.

As a general rule of thumb when working in Photoshop, you should have free disk space of at least 3.5 times the file size of the image you are working on. This is because Photoshop makes use of the Scratch disk as virtual memory and because Photoshop needs to hold more than one copy of the image you are working on for the Undo, Revert and From Saved commands.

HANDY TIP

Use the Plug-ins & Scratch Disk preferences (File > Preferences) to specify the hard disk you want Photoshop to use as a Scratch disk.

BEWARE

(Macintosh) Switch off Virtual Memory in the Memory control panel. Photoshop uses its own virtual memory management system to work with the Scratch disk.

Ruler Guides and Grids

You can show a grid in your image window to help with alignment and measuring, and you can also drag in ruler guides from the rulers. Both sets of guides are non-printing. You can customise the appearance of the grid and guides using File > Preferences > Guides & Grid.

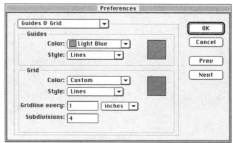

1 To hide or show the grid, choose View > Show / Hide Grid.

2 To create a ruler guide, first choose View > Show Rulers to display the rulers along the top and left edges of the image window. Then, position your cursor in a ruler and click and drag onto your image to create either a vertical or horizontal guide.

Make sure that Snap to Guides is selected in the View menu if you want cursors and selections to snap to guides and the grid. This is very useful for aligning elements accurately.

3 To reposition a ruler guide, select the Move tool, position your cursor on a guide, then click and drag. The cursor changes to a bi-directional arrow when you pick up a guide.

4 To remove a ruler guide, drag the ruler guide back into the ruler it came from. Alternatively, choose View > Clear Guides to remove all guides.

Moving Around

Use any combination of the Navigator palette, the zoom tool, the hand tool and the scroll bars for moving around and zooming in and out of your image.

1 Choose Window > Show Navigator to show the Navigator palette. In the palette, you can double-click the % entry box, enter a zoom % (0.198 – 1600%), then press Return/Enter.

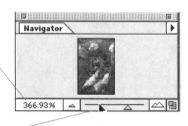

Alternatively, drag the zoom slider to the right to zoom in, or to the left to zoom out. Each time you change your zoom level, the view in the Proxy Preview area updates.

HANDY TIP

Hold down Command/ Ctrl and the spacebar to temporarily access the zoom tool with any other tool selected. Add the Alt/Option key (Mac) or the Alt key (Windows) to the above combination to zoom out.

2 Drag the red box in the Proxy Preview area to move quickly to different areas of your image.

3 To use the zoom tool, select it, position your cursor on the image and click to zoom in on the area around your cursor, in preset increments. With the zoom tool selected, hold down Alt/Option (Mac) or Alt (Windows). The cursor changes to the zoom out cursor; click to zoom out in the preset increments.

4 With the zoom tool selected, you can also click and drag to define the area you want to zoom in on.

HANDY TIP

With any other tool selected, hold down the spacebar to temporarily access the hand tool.

5 You can use the hand tool in addition to using the scroll bars to move around your image when you have zoomed in on it. Select the tool, position your cursor on the image, then click and drag to reposition.

The Info Palette

The Info palette (Window > Show Info) provides useful numerical read-outs relative to the position of the cursor on your image.

You can use it as an on-screen densitometer to examine colour values at the cursor. There are two colour read-outs. As a default, the first colour read-out is the actual colour under the cursor. For example, a read-out of red, green, and blue colour components in an RGB image. The second read-out as a default is for cyan, magenta, yellow and black values.

An exclamation mark next to the CMYK readouts indicates that a colour is out of gamut.

You also get x and y coordinates, giving the precise location of the cursor as it moves over the image.

If you create a selection, there is a read-out of the width and height of the selection. The palette also displays values for some options such as rotating, skewing and scaling selections.

1 To change the default settings for the Info Palette, choose Palette Options from the pop-up menu.

2 Use the Mode pop-ups to choose the first and second colour read-outs.

3 You can also choose a unit of measurement for mouse coordinates.

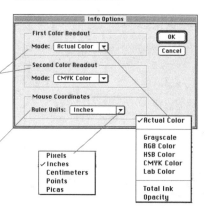

Palette Techniques

There are ten floating palettes in Photoshop. These movable palettes appear in front of images. Initially the palettes are grouped together. The default groupings for the palettes are Navigator-Info-Options, Colour-Swatches-Brushes, Layers-Channels-Paths-Actions.

This page uses Macintosh and Windows screen shots to illustrate the degree of similarity in functionality between the Windows and Macintosh platforms.

1 You can show any of the palette groups by selecting the appropriate palette from the Window menu. To close a palette, click on the Close box (Mac) or Close icon (Windows) in the title bar of each palette.

2 To move a palette, simply position your cursor in the title bar, then click and drag.

3 To choose a particular palette, click on the appropriate tab just below the title bar. You can drag these tabs to create separate palettes. Alternatively, you can drag a tab into another palette to create your own custom groupings of palettes.

4 You can shrink or roll up palettes to make the most of your available screen space. Click the Zoom box (Mac) or Minimise icon (Windows) in the title bar of the palette. Repeat the procedure to restore the palette to its original size. (You have to click twice on the Zoom/Minimise icon if the palette has been resized.)

...contd

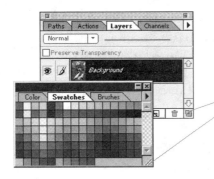

5 You can use standard Macintosh and Windows techniques to resize the Swatches and Brushes, Navigator, Layers, Channels, Actions and Paths palettes by dragging.

6 You can collapse some of the palettes to show title bar and tabs only, by double-clicking a tab. Repeat the procedure to restore the palette to its original size.

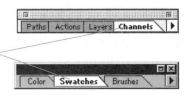

7 Press the Tab key to hide/show all palettes including the toolbox. Hold down Shift, then press Tab to hide/show currently visible palettes, with the exception of the toolbox.

8 You can restore the default settings for a tool by choosing Reset Tool from the pop-up menu in the tool options palette. Choose Reset All Tools to restore default settings for all tools.

9 All palettes have a pop-up menu for accessing a range of commands or options relevant to the palette.

Click and hold on the triangle (Mac), or just click the triangle (Windows).

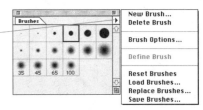

Saving and Loading Custom Settings

The Swatches, Brushes and Actions palettes, along with many dialogue boxes, such as Duotones, Levels and Curves, have Save and Load options which allow you to save custom settings you have made to the palette or dialogue box and then load them into the same image, or into other Photoshop images.

When you save settings, you are creating a file which stores the custom information. The example below is for the Brushes palette.

HANDY TIP

It's a good idea to set up a folder within your Adobe folder, or any other appropriate location, for saving your own custom settings. This means you will always be able to access and load the settings quickly and conveniently whenever you need them.

1 When you have customised the Brushes palette (see pages 66–67 and 78), choose Save Brushes in the pop-up menu (click the Save button in dialogue boxes) to save the changes.

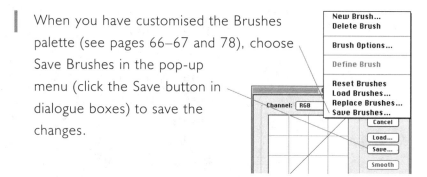

2 The Save Brushes In dialogue box prompts you for a file name and location in which to save the settings.

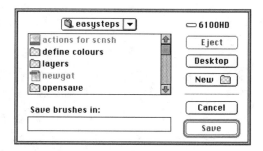

...contd

HANDY TIP

Look in the Goodies folder (Mac) or PH4 folder (Windows) for palettes that come with Photoshop. Try the Assorted Brushes as a starting point for experimenting with brush types.

3 To load settings that you have previously saved, choose Load Brushes in the pop-up (click on the Load button in a dialogue box), then specify the location of the settings you previously saved. Click on the name, then click Open/OK to load the settings.

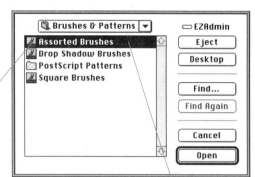

4 You can use the Reset option in the pop-up menu to restore settings to their original defaults.

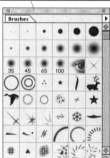

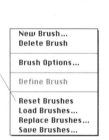

Understanding Histograms

A histogram represents the tonal range in an image – in other words, the spread or distribution of pixels through the highlight, midtone and shadow regions of the image. Histograms are useful as they provide a visual representation of the tonal balance of an image.

An 8-bit greyscale image contains 256 vertical bars, from 0 (black) to 255 (white). The height of each bar indicates the number of pixels the image contains for that grey level. In RGB images you can view a combined histogram which represents the overall brightness values, or you can use the channel pop-up to view the histogram for each channel (red, green, blue) in the image.

In an image with good colour balance you typically see an even distribution of pixels across the X axis.

An image lacking pixels in the highlight and shadow areas would be visually flat, lacking in contrast.

1 Choose Image > Histogram to view the histogram for an image.

Histogram

Channel: Luminosity

OK

Mean: 133.70   Level: 19
Std Dev: 63.38   Count: 291
Median: 151   Percentile: 4.54
Pixels: 90000

2 The Y axis represents the number of pixels for each grey level in the image.

3 The X axis runs from 0–255.

4 The readout along the bottom of the dialogue box indicates the number of pixels in the image depending on where the cursor is positioned along the X axis.

Opening and Saving Files

Chapter Three

Adobe Photoshop began life with the primary purpose of converting image formats for use on different applications and platforms. Since then it has gone on to become a market-leading image-editing application. This chapter covers the basic techniques of opening and saving images in Photoshop.

Covers

Opening Images in Photoshop

Once you have launched Photoshop you can open images using the File menu. Some specialist file formats open using the File > Import command.

1 To open a picture from within Photoshop, choose File > Open. This takes you into the Open File dialogue box.

2 Navigate through folders and sub-folders as necessary to locate the file you wish to open, click on

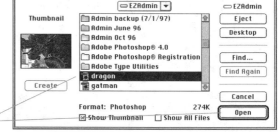

the file name to select it, then click Open. Alternatively, just double-click the file name.

HANDY TIP

Click the Create button if it is available for Photoshop to create a thumbnail preview of the file you have selected in the file list box.

3 Use the Show Thumbnail option either to hide or to show the thumbnail area to the left of the dialogue box. Select the Show All Files option to access a pop-up menu that will allow

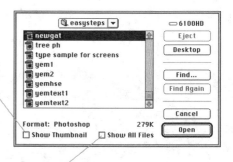

you to specify in which format you want to open a file. In Windows you can use the Open As command to open a file that has a missing or incorrect file extension.

HANDY TIP

Double-click Photoshop file icons in the Windows or Macintosh file-management environments to open the file. If Photoshop is not running, this will also launch Photoshop.

4 In Windows you can choose from the most recently opened files in the File menu.

Scanning into Photoshop

You can scan into Photoshop either using the TWAIN interface, using a scanner plug-in designed for use with Photoshop, or, if your scanner does not have a plug-in for Photoshop, you can use the scanner software to scan the image, save the image in TIFF, PICT or BMP format, then open the file in Photoshop.

BEWARE

Make sure the plug-in for your scanner is in Photoshop's Import/Export plug-ins folder. Plug-in modules for installed scanners appear in the File > Import submenu.

1 The first time you scan into Photoshop using the TWAIN interface, choose File > TWAIN Select. Locate your scanner, select the scanner icon and click OK to specify the scanner.

2 Choose File > TWAIN Acquire. This takes you into your scanning software.

Anti-aliased PICT...
PICT Resource...
Quick Edit...
Twain Acquire...
Twain Select...

Refer to your scanning software manual for details of the controls available. Typically, you can choose settings for scan mode (greyscale, colour, line art etc.), resolution, scale, contrast, brightness and gamma settings.

Many of the scanning controls have equivalent functions in Photoshop. Scanning options vary from scanner to scanner, but you should be able to specify whether you are scanning a transparency or a photograph. The other essential decisions you need to make at this stage are mode, resolution and scale. You will also need to specify a crop area in the preview window.

Mode:	Gray-Scale
Original:	Reflective
Output:	200 ppi
Scale To:	100%
Range:	Automatic
Tone Curve:	Gamma 1.8
Descreen:	None
Sharpness:	None
Preferences:	General
Settings:	Current

HANDY TIP

If your scanner does not have a plug-in for Photoshop, use the scanner software to scan the image, save the image in TIFF, PICT or BMP format, then open it in Photoshop.

3 Click the scan button. Wait until the scanning process finishes and the image appears in an untitled Photoshop window. Save the image.

Opening Photo CD Images

Photo CD files are found inside the Images folder within the Photo CD folder.

The Photo CD format, developed by Kodak, uses the YCC colour model. This is becoming a more and more popular method for creating and storing digital images.

The YCC colour model provides an extremely broad range of colour. When you open a Photo CD image in Photoshop, you translate the YCC image to Photoshop's Lab colour or RGB mode using a 'Precision Transform'. The precision transforms are designed to convert images accurately, preserving the colour values of the original.

1   To open a Photo CD Image, choose File > Open. Select the image you want to open and click OK. The Photo CD Plug-in dialogue box appears.

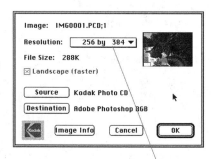

2   Use the Resolution pop-up menu to choose a resolution from 128 x 192 pixels (72k, 2.667 by 1.778 inches) to 2,048 x 3,072 pixels (18Mb, 42.668 by 28.445 inches). In this case, resolution refers to the dimensions of the image in pixels. All Photo CD images open in Photoshop at a resolution of 72 pixels per inch.

3   Click the Image Info button. The dialogue box gives information about the image and the medium of

A product type of O52/55 denotes Universal Ektachrome, while 116/22 denotes Universal Kodachrome.

the original. Make a note of the medium of the original – whether it was a colour negative or slide (Colour Reversal). For a Colour Reversal, make a note of the 'Product Type of Original'. You will use this information in the Source option to select the appropriate Precision Transform for a specific Photo CD image. OK the Image Info box.

...contd

4 Click the Source button. Choose Kodak Photo CD from the Source Device pop-up menu, then choose a description according to the Product Type of Original you noted in the Image Info box. In this example the choice is Universal Ektachrome. If the Medium of Original is Colour Reversal, but you don't know the film type, use Universal Kodachrome. OK the dialogue box.

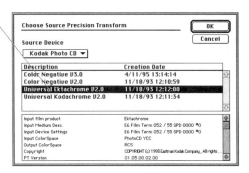

5 Click the Destination button. Use the Destination Device pop-up menu to select Adobe Photoshop RGB or CIELAB. OK the dialogue box.

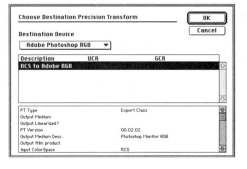

6 OK the Photo CD Plug-in dialogue box. The image will open in Photoshop.

Opening an EPS File

EPS files, which are created in applications such as Adobe Illustrator and Macromedia FreeHand, can contain object-oriented or 'vector' format information. When you open an EPS file in Photoshop, it is rasterized: that is, the vector information is converted into Photoshop's pixel-based format.

1 To open an EPS file as a new document, choose File > Open. Locate and highlight an EPS picture to be opened, then click the Open button. Alternatively, double-click the file name.

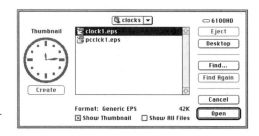

2 In the Rasterize dialogue box, choose a unit of measurement from the pop-up menus next to the height and width fields, and enter new dimensions if required.

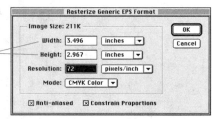

3 Enter the resolution required for your final output device and choose an image mode from the Mode pop-up menu.

4 Select the Constrain Proportions box to keep the original proportions of the EPS. Select Anti-aliased to slightly blur pixels along edges to avoid unwanted jagged edges.

5 Click OK. The EPS appears in its own image window. It is now a bitmap image.

Placing an EPS File

You can also 'place' an Illustrator or FreeHand EPS file into an open Photoshop document.

Before you place an EPS into Photoshop, it's a good idea to choose File > Preferences > General, then check the Anti-alias PostScript box. This preference helps create a smooth result.

1 To place an EPS file into an existing Photoshop file, first open a picture in Photoshop.

2 Choose File > Place. Use the Place Document dialogue box to specify the location and name of the EPS file, then click Place.

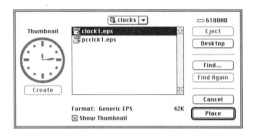

3 A bounding box with eight 'handles' and a cross through the placed image will appear on your Photoshop image. The EPS image itself may take a few seconds to draw inside the bounding box.

4 Drag a corner handle to resize the placed image. Hold down Shift as you drag to maintain proportions. Position your cursor inside the bounding box of the placed image and drag to reposition the image.

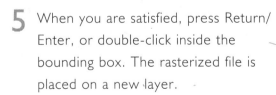

If you don't want to accept the placed image, press the Esc key. If you have already placed the image you will have to delete the new layer. (See page 106.)

5 When you are satisfied, press Return/ Enter, or double-click inside the bounding box. The rasterized file is placed on a new layer.

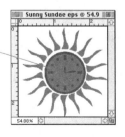

Saving Files

To create a thumbnail icon that will display in the thumbnail area of the Open dialogue box, choose File > Preferences > Saving Files. Select Always Save from the Image Previews pop-up, then click the Thumbnail option.

The basic principles of saving files in Photoshop – using 'Save' and 'Save As' – are the same as in any other Macintosh or Windows application. You should save regularly as you make changes to an image so that you do not lose work you have done if a system crash occurs. You should use Save As to save a new file in the first instance and to make copies of a file.

Photoshop supports numerous file formats for opening and saving images. Typically, you save an image in a particular format either to meet specific output or printing specifications, to compress the image to save disk space, or to open or import the image into an application that requires a particular file format.

1 To save an image in the first instance, choose File > Save As. Specify where you want to save the file. Enter a name for the file. Use the Format pop-up to choose an appropriate format. Click on the Save button.

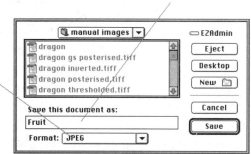

To create image icons for the Finder on the Macintosh, choose File > Preferences > Saving Files. Select Always Save from the Image Previews pop-up, then click the Icon option.

2 To save changes that you have made to an image that you are working on, choose File > Save. The previously saved file is updated.

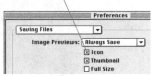

Photoshop Format

This is sometimes referred to as native format: use this format as you work on your image. Applications such as QuarkXPress will not import images in Photoshop format, but all of Photoshop's options, in particular layers, remain available to you when you save in this format. Photoshop also performs open and save routines more quickly when using its native format.

TIFFs

TIFF (Tagged Image File Format), originally developed by Aldus, became a standard file format for scanned images in the early days of desktop publishing, and is common on both Mac and Windows platforms.

To save an image in TIFF format, choose File > Save As. The Save As dialogue box appears.

On the Macintosh, use the Saving Files preferences dialogue box to specify whether or not you want file extensions – e.g. '.tif' – automatically added when saving files.

Specify where you want to save the image and enter a name in the name entry box. Use the Format pop-up menu to choose TIFF, then click OK.

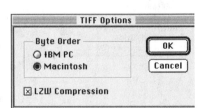

The TIFF options dialogue box will appear. Select Byte Order options and LZW Compression as required, then OK the dialogue box.

Byte Order

Use this option to specify whether you want the TIFF to be used on a Mac or a PC, as Mac and PC TIFF formats vary slightly.

LZW Compression

(Lempel-Ziv-Welch) is a compression format that looks for repeated elements in the computer code that describes the image and replaces these with shorter sequences. Most importantly, this is a 'lossless' compression scheme (i.e., none of the image's detail is lost). Applications such as QuarkXPress, Adobe PageMaker and Macromedia FreeHand can import TIFFs with LZW compression.

Photoshop EPS

EPS is generally more reliable for PostScript printing than TIFF file format, but generates file sizes which can be three to four times greater than TIFFs with LZW compression. To save in EPS format, do the following:

| . Follow the procedure for saving TIFFs, but choose Photoshop EPS from the Format pop-up menu. Click OK. The EPS format dialogue box will appear. Specify your settings, then click OK.

Preview

This option specifies the quality of the low-resolution screen preview you see when you import the image into applications such as Adobe PageMaker and QuarkXPress. Use

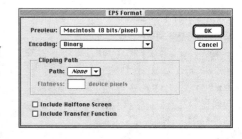

'Macintosh (8bits/pixel)' for a colour preview. 'Macintosh (JPEG)' uses JPEG compression routines, but is only supported by Postscript Level 2 printers. Use TIFF if you want to use the image in Windows.

Encoding

Use binary encoding if you want to export the image for use with Adobe Illustrator. Some applications do not recognise binary encoding; in this case you have to use ASCII.

Clipping Path

Use the Path pop-up menu to select a path you have previously created in the image to become a clipping path. The clipping path acts as a mask on the EPS image when you import it into applications such as QuarkXPress and Adobe PageMaker. (See pages 134–135.)

JPEG

JPEG is an acronym for Joint Photo-graphic Experts Group. It is an extremely efficient compression format and is frequently used for images on the World Wide Web. JPEG format is available when saving greyscale, RGB and CMYK images.

The JPEG compression routine is a 'lossy' procedure. To make the file size of the image smaller, image data is discarded, resulting in reduced image quality.

1 Follow the procedure for saving in TIFF format, but choose JPEG from the Format pop-up menu.

2 Use the Quality pop-up to specify the amount of compression, or drag the slider. Maximum gives best image quality, retaining most of the detail in an image, but uses the least compression. Low gives lowest image quality, but uses maximum compression.

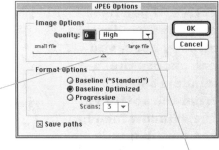

3 In the Format Options area, select Baseline Optimised to optimise the colour quality of the image.

JPEG is a cumulative compression scheme – if you close an image, then reopen it and save it in JPEG format, you will apply a further compression to the image, effectively losing more colour information from the image. Save to JPEG format only after you finish all work on an image.

4 Select Progressive and enter a value for Scans if you intend to use the image on the World Wide Web. This option downloads the image in a series of passes which add detail to the image progressively.

5 Select the Save Paths option to save any paths in the image when you save the file.

Creating a New File

When you need a fresh, completely blank canvas to work on, you should create a new file.

HANDY TIP

Whilst the New dialogue box is active, if you have an image window already open, you can choose the window's name from the bottom of the Window menu; the new dialogue box will update with the settings from the file you selected.

1 To create a new file, choose File > New. Enter a name for the new document (or leave this as Untitled and do a Save As later).

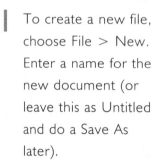

2 Specify width and height settings. If you have copied or cut pixels to the clipboard, the width and height fields automatically reflect the dimensions of the elements on the clipboard.

3 Enter a resolution and choose a colour mode.

4 Select one of the contents options to specify the canvas background you want to begin with, then OK the dialogue box.

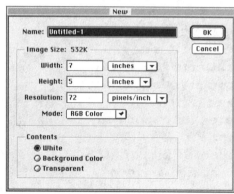

HANDY TIP

You can use the Fill command to fill selections with colour.

5 To change the colour of the canvas, select a foreground colour (see Chapter Five, 'Defining Colours'). Next, choose Edit > Fill. Choose Foreground from the Use pop-up, then OK the dialogue box.

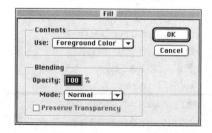

Getting Started with Images

There are a number of common techniques and tasks, such as cropping the image and making it larger or smaller, or changing the resolution to suit your final output needs, that you need to undertake on many of the images on which you work. This chapter covers a range of these tasks.

Covers

Chapter Four

Rotating an Image

You can quickly rotate an image if you have scanned it at the wrong orientation, or, for example, if you have opened a Photo CD image using the Landscape option.

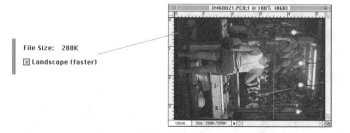

File Size: 288K
☒ Landscape (faster)

To rotate an image in set increments, use Image > Rotate Canvas. Choose one of the preset increments. CW stands for clockwise, CCW for counter-clockwise. In the example above, you would choose 90 degrees counter-clockwise to rotate the Beijing Duck seller upright.

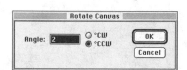

HANDY TIP

When using arbitrary rotation, position a ruler guide (see page 25, 'Ruler Guides and Grids') to help determine how far you need to rotate.

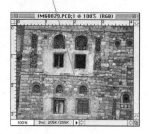

Sometimes you need to adjust an image a few degrees to make up for a poor original photograph or slightly misaligned scan:

2 To rotate in precise amounts, choose Image > Rotate Canvas > Arbitrary. Enter a value for the rotation. Choose the clockwise or counter-clockwise radio button, then OK the dialogue box.

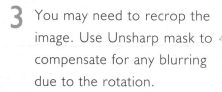

3 You may need to recrop the image. Use Unsharp mask to compensate for any blurring due to the rotation.

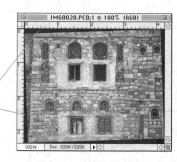

Resizing without Resampling

REMEMBER

When you make the image smaller without resampling, the pixels get smaller. Effectively, you are increasing the resolution of the image. When you make an image bigger without resampling, the pixels get larger and this can lead to jagged, blocky results. Effectively, you are reducing the resolution of the image.

When you resize an image without resampling, you make the image larger or smaller without changing the total number of pixels in the image. The overall dimensions of the image change, the file size remains the same, but the resolution of the image goes up if you make the image smaller, down if you make the image larger.

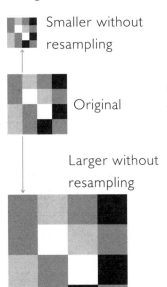

Smaller without resampling

Original

Larger without resampling

1 To decrease the size of your image without resampling, choose Image > Image Size. Make sure that Resample Image is deselected. Enter a lower value in the Width or Height entry box. The other measurement updates automatically. The file size of the image remains the same – no pixels have been added. The resolution has increased – the same number of pixels are packed into a smaller area.

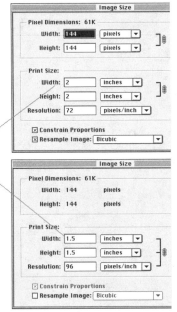

2 To increase the size of your image without resampling, enter a higher value in the Width or Height entry box. The file size of the image remains the same, but the resolution has decreased.

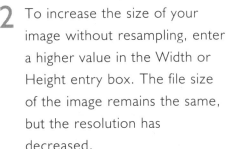

Resampling Up

Resampling up involves interpolation. Interpolation is used when Photoshop has to add information – new pixels – that didn't previously exist to an image. There are three methods to choose from the pop-up in the Image size dialogue box. Bicubic gives best results, but takes longest; Nearest Neighbour is quickest, but least accurate.

When you resample up, new pixels are added to the image, so file size increases. Resampling takes place when you increase the resolution setting, or the width/height setting with the Resample Image option selected.

The examples here start with a 2 in by 2 in image at 72 ppi.

Choose Image > Image Size. To keep the overall dimensions of the image, but increase the resolution, make sure that Resample Image is selected. Select Constrain Proportions so that the image's original proportions are maintained. Enter a higher value in the Resolution box.

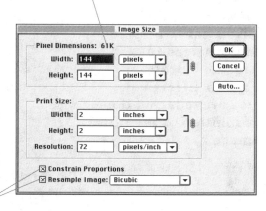

HANDY TIP

To reset the dialogue box to its original settings, hold down Alt/ Option (Mac) or Alt (Windows), then click the Reset button.

2 The file size and total number of pixels increase, but the width and height dimensions remain the same.

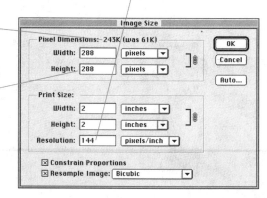

...contd

You now have an image which is the same overall size, but which has more pixels in the same area, and therefore its resolution is increased:

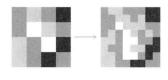

 When you resample an image, blurring may occur due to the process of interpolation. Use the Unsharp Mask filter to compensate for this. (See pages 171–172.)

3 To make the overall size/dimensions of the image bigger, but to keep the same resolution, again make sure that Resample Image is selected. Select Constrain Proportions to keep width and height proportional. Enter a higher value in either the width or height entry boxes. (The other entry box will update automatically if you have selected Constrain Proportions.)

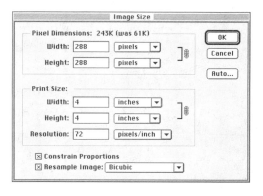

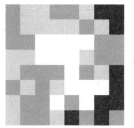

4 The overall dimensions of the image have now increased. The file size and total number of pixels have also increased, but the resolution remains the same.

Sampling Down

You sometimes need to resample down to maintain an optimal balance between the resolution needed for acceptable final output and file size considerations. There is little point in working with an image at too high a resolution if some of the image information is redundant at final output.

Resampling down means discarding pixels. The result is a smaller file size. Resampling down occurs when you decrease the resolution setting, or the width/ height setting with Resample Image option selected.

These examples start with a 2 in by 2 in image at 300 ppi.

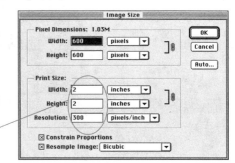

1 Choose Image > Image Size. To keep the overall dimensions of the image, but decrease the resolution, make sure that Resample Image is selected. Leave Constrain Proportions selected, so that the image's original proportions are maintained. Reduce the value in the Resolution box.

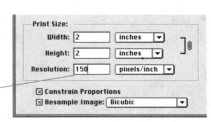

2 The file size goes down and the total number of pixels decreases, whilst the width and height dimensions remain the same.

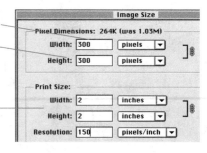

You now have an image which is the same overall size, but with fewer pixels in the same area, and therefore its resolution is decreased:

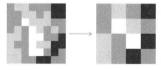  

3 To reduce the overall dimensions of the image, but keep the image at the same resolution, again make sure that Resample Image is selected. (Select Constrain Proportions to keep the width and height proportional.) Enter a lower value in either the width or height entry box.

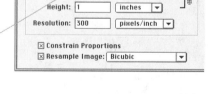

(The other entry box will update automatically if you have selected Constrain Proportions.)

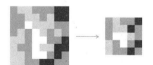

4 The overall dimensions of the image have now decreased. The file size and the total number of pixels have also decreased, but the resolution remains the same.

Cropping an Image

Use the Crop tool to crop unwanted areas of an image and reduce the file size.

Press C on the keyboard to select the Crop tool, then press Return/Enter to show the Crop tool options palette.

1 Select the Crop tool from the Marquee group. You can double-click the tool to show the Crop tool options palette.

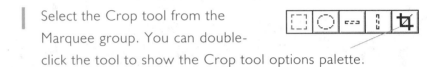

2 Position your cursor on the image, then click and drag to define the crop area. Don't worry if you don't get the crop exactly right first time.

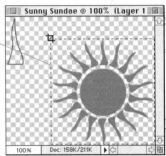

3 • To reposition the crop marquee, place your cursor inside the marquee, then click and drag.

   • To resize the crop marquee, place your cursor on one of the 8 handles around the marquee (the cursor changes to a bi-directional arrow), then click and drag.

   • To rotate the marquee, position your cursor just outside the marquee (the cursor changes shape to indicate rotation), then click and drag in a circular direction.

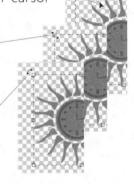

Hold down Shift, then click and drag on a corner handle to resize the crop marquee in proportion.

4 When you are satisfied with the position and size of the crop marquee, press Return (Mac) or Enter (Windows) to crop the picture. Alternatively, you can double-click inside the crop marquee. The areas outside the marquee are discarded. Press the Esc key if you do not want to accept the crop marquee.

Adding a Border

Borders are useful when you need additional space around the edges of your image.

BEWARE

Make sure that you select a background colour for your border, before you use the Canvas Size dialogue box.

1 Choose Image > Canvas Size. Use the measurement pop-up menus to choose a unit of measurement. Enter increased values for the width and/or height fields.

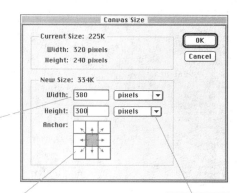

percent
pixels
• inches
cm
points
picas

2 To specify where the border is added relative to the image, click one of the white placement squares. This sets the relative position of the image and the border. The grey square represents the position of the image, the white squares the position of the border.

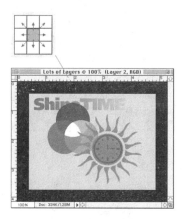

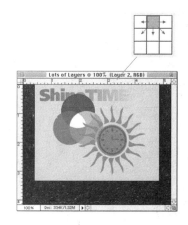

3 OK the dialogue and the border is added, filled with the background colour.

Image Modes

```
Bitmap
Grayscale
Duotone
Indexed Color...
✓RGB Color
CMYK Color
Lab Color
Multichannel

✓8 Bits/Channel
16 Bits/Channel

Color Table...
```

Image modes are fundamental to working in Photoshop. When you open an image the mode is indicated in the title bar of the image window. There are eight different modes in Photoshop; some overlap in what they have to offer, others are used for specific purposes. Use modes as appropriate to your working requirements. Then, depending on output or printing requirements, if necessary, convert to a different mode.

RGB Mode

Images are typically scanned or captured in RGB mode. When you start work with a colour image it is usually best to work in RGB mode, as this is faster than CMYK mode and allows you to use all of Photoshop's commands and features, providing greatest flexibility.

The disadvantage of working in RGB mode, if your image will be printed, is that RGB allows a greater gamut of colours than you can print. At some stage, some of the brightest, most vibrant colours will lose their brilliance when the image is brought within the CMYK gamut.

CMYK Mode

Convert to CMYK when the image is to be printed and you have finished making changes.

To place a colour image in a page layout application from where it will be colour separated, you need to convert from RGB to CMYK. When you convert from RGB to CMYK, Photoshop adjusts any colours in the RGB image that fall outside the CMYK gamut to their nearest printable colour. (See Chapter Five, 'Defining Colours', for details on gamut warnings.)

You can retain the flexibility of working in RGB mode, but see an on-screen CMYK preview of your image, by choosing View > CMYK Preview. (You may have to wait a few seconds when you choose this option as Photoshop builds its colour conversion tables.)

...contd

You can also select Display out of Gamut colours from the View menu, to highlight in grey areas of the image that are out of gamut.

Indexed Colour Mode
This mode reduces your image to 256 colours or less and is frequently used for multimedia and Web images. (See Chapter Sixteen, 'Web and Multimedia Images'.)

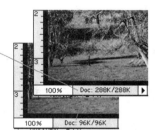

Duotone
For details on using Duotone mode see the following page.

Greyscale Mode
When you are not printing an image in colour you can convert to greyscale mode to make working faster and file size smaller.

Lab Mode
This mode uses the CIE Lab mode which has one channel for luminosity, an 'a' channel representing colours blue to yellow, a 'b' channel for magenta to green. A significant advantage to this mode is that its gamut encompasses that of both CMYK and RGB modes.

Bitmap Mode
This mode reduces everything to black or white pixels. The image becomes a one-bit image.

To convert from one mode to another choose Image > Mode and choose the mode you want from the submenu. Depending on which mode you are converting from and to, you may get a message box warning you of any consequences of converting to the new mode and asking you to confirm your request.

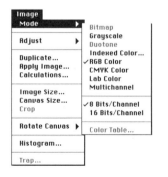

REMEMBER You must first convert to greyscale mode before you can convert to Duotone mode.

Duotone Mode

You can only access Duotone mode when you have converted to greyscale.

Duotone is a very popular effect used to give added tonal depth to a greyscale image by printing with black and another colour.

I To create a duotone, choose Image > Mode > Duotone. The Duotone dialogue box appears. Choose from the pop-up whether you want to create a duotone (two inks), a tritone (three inks) or a quadtone (four inks).

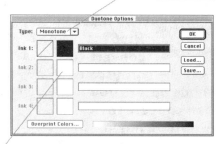

When you start working with Photoshop, click on the Load button and try using one of the preset duotone settings that can be found in: Adobe Photoshop > Goodies > Duotone Presets > Duotones.

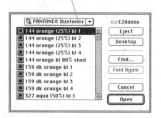

2 To choose a second colour for the duotone, click the 'Ink 2' box below the black ink box. This takes you into the Custom Colours dialogue box. Choose a colour. Click the Picker button if you want to use the Colour Picker. OK the dialogue box.

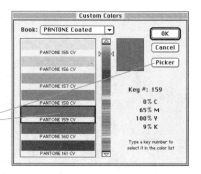

Make sure you save duotones in EPS format so that they colour separate correctly from page layout applications.

3 To specify the ink coverage for both colours, click on the Ink I Curve icon. This takes you into the Duotone Curve dialogue box. Drag the curve to the desired position, or enter values in the % entry boxes to adjust the ink coverage curve. OK both dialogue boxes to see the result.

Defining Colours

Defining colours is an essential aspect of using Photoshop and there is a range of techniques that can be used. The colour controls in the Tool palette indicate the current foreground and background colours.

Chapter Five

Covers

Foreground and Background Colours

The foreground colour is applied when you create type, and when you use the Paint bucket, Line, Pencil, Airbrush and Paintbrush tools.

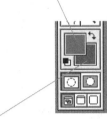

The background colour is the colour you get when you use the Eraser tool, or when you delete or move a selection.

When you are working with foreground and background controls you can also switch colours, and you can quickly change back to the default colours, black and white.

You can change the background and foreground colours using the Eyedropper tool, the Colour Picker palette, the Colour palette and the Swatches palette.

HANDY TIP

Press X on the keyboard to switch background and foreground colours.

1 To switch background to foreground and vice versa, click once on the Switch Colours arrow.

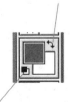

2 To revert to black and white as the default background and foreground colours, click the Default colours icon.

The Eyedropper Tool (I)

The Eyedropper tool provides a quick and convenient way to pick up foreground and background colour from an area of the image you are working on, or from another inactive Photoshop image window.

1 To set the foreground colour, click once on the Eyedropper tool.

2 Position your cursor, then click once on the image. Notice that the foreground box in the Toolbox now represents the colour where you clicked.

3 To set the background colour, hold down Alt/Option (Mac) or Alt (Windows), then click on the image. The background box in the Toolbox now indicates the colour where you clicked.

You can use the Eyedropper Options palette (Window > Show Options) to specify the sample area of the image that the Eyedropper picks up.

HANDY TIP

Double-click the Eyedropper tool to show the Eyedropper Options palette if it is not already showing.

4 To set the Sample Size, use the Sample Size pop-up menu to choose a value. Point size reads the precise value of the pixel on which you click. 3 by 3 and 5 by 5 take average values of the pixels where you click.

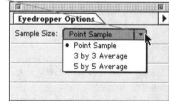

The Colour Picker Palette

One of the most powerful and flexible ways of choosing foreground and background colours is using the Colour Picker palette. You can use a number of different colour models to create colour.

> To create a CMYK colour using the Colour Picker, click once on either the foreground or background colour box. The Colour Picker dialogue box will appear.

Press the Tab key to move the highlight through the entry boxes in the dialogue box.

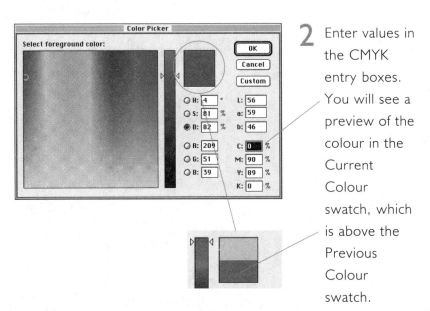

2 Enter values in the CMYK entry boxes. You will see a preview of the colour in the Current Colour swatch, which is above the Previous Colour swatch.

3 OK the dialogue box when you have mixed the colour you want. This now becomes the foreground or background colour, depending on which box you clicked in step 1.

...contd

You can also create colours using the Colour Slider and the Colour field. The next example looks at creating a colour using Hue, Saturation and Brightness values. You can apply the same techniques to Red, Green, Blue (RGB) and Lab colour models.

1 To create a colour using Hue, Saturation and Brightness (HSB) values, first click the Hue radio button.

2 Click on the Colour Slider bar, or drag the slider triangles on either side of the bar, to choose a hue or colour. This sets one of the three HSB values. The

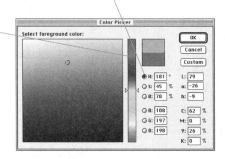

Hue entry box changes to a number that represents the hue you have chosen (0–360).

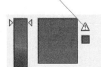

A warning triangle – the Gamut alarm – will appear next to the Current/ Previous colour boxes if you create a colour that cannot be printed using CMYK inks. Click the warning triangle to choose the nearest printable colour. The small box below the warning triangle indicates the nearest printable colour.

3 Next, click in the Colour Field to set the other two variables – Saturation and Brightness. Clicking to the left of the field reduces the saturation, clicking to the right increases the saturation of the selected hue. Clicking near the bottom decreases brightness, clicking near the top increases brightness for the selected hue.

4 If you click on the Saturation button, the Colour Slider now represents saturation (from 0–100) and the colour field allows you to choose Hue and Brightness values. When you click the Brightness radio button, the slider represents Brightness and the colour field represents Hue and Saturation.

Selecting Pantone Colours

You can access a range of colour-matching systems using the Colour Picker dialogue box. These include: Toyo Colour Finder 1050 System, Focoltone Colour System, Pantone Matching System, Trumatch Swatching System and DIC Colour Guide. Here, we'll select a Pantone colour.

1 To select a Pantone colour, click the foreground or background colour box. The Colour Picker dialogue box will appear. Click the Custom button.

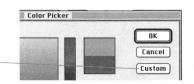

2 Use the Book pop-up menu to select a Pantone matching system.

3 If you know the Pantone number of the colour you want, you can enter the number on the keyboard. Alternatively, click in the colour slider bar to the right of the Pantone colour boxes.

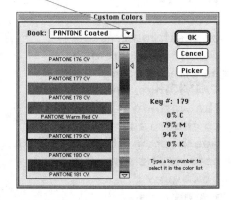

This moves you to a general range of colours. Then click on the scroll bars at the top and bottom of the sliders to find the specific Pantone colour you want.

4 Click on the colour you want to select, then click OK.

The Colour Palette

You can also use the Colour palette to choose colours (Window > Show Colours).

If you click the active colour selection box, you will display the Colour Picker palette.

1 First identify which colour selection box is 'active'. There are two boxes, foreground and background. The active box is outlined by a black line.

2 Continue with step 3 if the correct box is active, or click the inactive box to make it the active box if necessary.

During step 3, if you create a colour that is outside the CMYK colour gamut, the gamut alert warning triangle appears. You can click on the alert triangle to set the colour to the nearest CMYK equivalent. The nearest CMYK equivalent appears in a box next to the alert triangle.

3 Drag the colour slider triangles below the colour slider bars, or enter values in the entry boxes to the right of the palette. You can also click on a colour in the Colour Bar running along the bottom of the Colour palette. The Colour Bar contains every colour in the CMYK spectrum as a default setting.

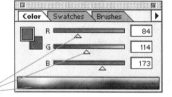

4 Use the pop-up triangle in the top right of the palette to change the colour model for sliders. Choose from Greyscale, RGB, HSB, CMYK, LAB sliders.

Grayscale Slider
✓RGB Sliders
HSB Sliders
CMYK Sliders
Lab Sliders

Color Bar...

Hold down Command (Mac) or Ctrl (Windows) and click the Colour bar to access the Colour Bar dialogue box.

5 You can also use the pop-up menu to change the Colour Bar setting. Choose Colour Bar..., then use the Style pop-up menu in the Colour Bar dialogue box to choose an option for the Colour Bar.

Color Bar

Style: CMYK Spectrum

RGB Spectrum
• CMYK Spectrum
Grayscale Ramp
Current Colors

OK

Cancel

The Swatches Palette

You can use the Swatches palette (Window > Show Swatches) to set foreground and background colours, and you can also use it to create custom palettes which you can save and then reload into a different image.

HANDY TIP

See page 30 for details on loading and saving custom palette settings.

1 To select a foreground colour from the Swatches palette, click on a colour swatch.

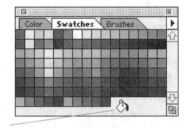

2 To select a background colour, hold down Alt/Option (Mac) or Alt (Windows) and then click on a colour swatch.

You can customise the Swatches palette by adding and deleting colours in the palette.

HANDY TIP

Shift-clicking on an existing swatch replaces it with the current foreground colour. Pressing Shift and then Alt/Option (Mac) or Alt (Windows) while clicking on a swatch inserts the current foreground colour to the left of the colour you click.

3 To add colour to the swatches, select a foreground colour. Position your cursor in an empty area of the Swatches palette. (The cursor changes to a paint bucket.) Then click to add the foreground colour.

4 To delete a colour swatch, hold down Command (Mac) or Ctrl (Windows) and then click on a colour swatch.

The Painting Tools

The Airbrush, Paintbrush, Pencil, Smudge and Line tools apply the foreground colour to pixels in your image as you drag across them. Each painting tool creates a painting stroke with different characteristics. You can use the Brushes palette to determine the shape, size and type of the brush stroke for the Airbrush, Paintbrush, Pencil and Smudge tools.

All the painting and editing tools can be used on a selection or anywhere on an image.

Covers

Chapter Six

The Brushes Palette

The Brushes palette is central to using the painting and editing tools. Before you use any of these tools you need to check your brush size and shape. Choose Window > Show Brushes to show the Brushes palette.

1 To choose a hard-edged brush, click a brush in the first row of the default palette. To use a soft-edged brush, click one of the brushes in the second row. (The circle icons in the first two rows represent the actual size of the brush.) The third row contains brushes that are too large to be represented at their actual size. The number below them is the diameter of the brush in pixels.

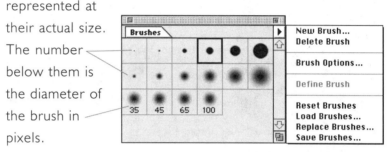

You can use Brush Options from the pop-up menu to edit the settings for a selected brush.

2 To create a new brush, choose New Brush from the pop-up menu. Enter values for Diameter, Hardness, Spacing, Angle and Roundness in the New Brush dialogue box.

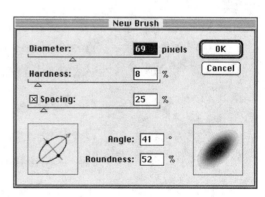

Diameter

Enter a value in pixels for the diameter of your brush from 1–999. Brush sizes too large to be represented at their actual size will display with the diameter indicated as a number.

...contd

Hardness

A setting of 100% gives a hard-edged brush. Settings below 100% produce soft-edged brushes. The lower you take this setting, the more diffuse the resultant stroke when you paint with the brush. Even with a setting of 100%, the edge of the brush-stroke is anti-aliased.

Spacing

Spacing is measured as a percentage of brush size. 25% is the default setting for all brushes. Higher settings begin to create non-continuous strokes.

Angle and Roundness

Use these controls together to create a stroke which thickens and thins like a calligraphic pen. You can enter values in the entry boxes, or drag the arrow indicator to change the angle, and drag the diameter dots to change the diameter.

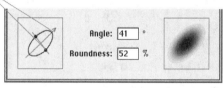

To delete a brush, click on it to select it, **then choose Delete brush in the pop-up menu.**

3 OK the dialogue box. The new brush is added to the palette. The keyline around it indicates that it is selected. (See page 30 for details on saving customised palettes for future use.)

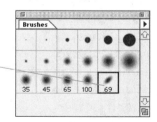

New Brush...
Delete Brush

Brush Options...

Define Brush

Reset Brushes
Load Brushes...
Replace Brushes...
Save Brushes...

Painting Tool Techniques and Settings

Each painting tool has its own Options palette. There is a range of Options palette settings and techniques common to many of the painting and editing tools. Use the options covered here in conjunction with the specific controls for each of the tools on the following pages.

With a tool selected, press Return/Enter to show its Options palette.

Opacity, Pressure and Exposure

Opacity (Paintbrush, Line, Pencil, Eraser, Rubber Stamp), Pressure (Airbrush, Smudge, Focus tools) and Exposure (Toning tools) have a similar effect and determine the intensity of the tool you are working with. For example, opacity controls how completely pixels are covered by the foreground colour when you drag across them.

Make sure the Opacity/Pressure slider is at 100% if you want to completely cover the pixels you drag across. (Soft-edged brushes only partially cover pixels around the edge of the painting stroke to create the soft edge effect.) Reducing the Opacity/Pressure setting gives less complete results in the area you drag across, creating a semi-transparent, partially-covered effect.

Number keys on the keyboard can be used to set Opacity in increments of 10. (0 = 100%, 1 = 10%, 2 = 20% etc.) You can type two numbers in quick succession to specify other percentages.

Fade

Use the Fade setting to create the effect of paint on the painting tool running out as you drag across the image. The rate of Fade controls the number of pixels that are coloured before the paint fades to nothing. The higher the Fade setting, the further the paint goes before it fades out completely.

1   To set a fade rate for the paintbrush, airbrush or pencil, double-click the tool to show the tool's Options palette.

2   Enter a fade value and use the Transparency/Background pop-up to specify what you want to fade to.

☒Fade: 20	steps to	Transparent ▾
Stylus Pressure: ☐Size		• Transparent
		Background

...contd

Undoing

To undo the last stroke you painted, choose Edit > Undo. This only works for the very last action you performed. In instances where you need to undo several steps, you can use File > Revert to revert to the version of the file when you last saved it.

Cursor Types

Press Caps Lock to change painting and editing tool cursors to precise crosshairs. This is a very useful technique for making fine adjustments.

2 Choose File > Preferences > Display and Cursors to change the way your painting tool cursors appear on-screen. 'Precise' has the same effect as pressing Caps Lock. 'Brush Size' is useful because you see the actual brush size represented on screen. (Changing the Painting Cursors preference to Precise reverses the effect of Caps Lock.)

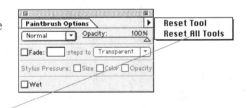

HANDY TIP

Whilst you are working with a painting tool, hold down Alt/Option (Mac) or Alt (Windows) to temporarily access the Eyedropper tool. This is useful for selecting a new foreground colour with which to paint.

Painting Tool Options Palettes

You can use the pop-up menu in each of the painting tool Options palettes to reset the default setting for the tool, or you can reset defaults for all tools.

The Paintbrush Tool (B)

The Paintbrush in Photoshop is like a normal paintbrush. You drag it across the pixels in your image and it colours those pixels with the foreground colour.

You can use a Fade setting to make the paint run out, just as with a normal paintbrush. You can also change the opacity setting to achieve a translucent, partial coverage of the pixels you drag across.

 Remember to choose an appropriate brush size and shape before you begin painting.

To paint with the Paintbrush, Line, Pencil or Airbrush, first double-click the tool to show the Options palette for that tool if it is not already showing.

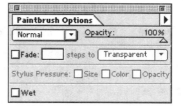

2 Choose the settings you want, then position your cursor on the image, click and drag.

 To constrain your painting strokes to straight lines, click with the painting tool to position the start of the stroke, move your cursor, (do not click and drag), then hold down Shift and click to end the stroke.

Wet (Paintbrush & Eraser)

When you paint with wet edges selected you get a stroke that is darker around the edges and translucent inside the stroke, imitating the uneven build-up of paint in a watercolour.

The Airbrush Tool (A)

Use the Airbrush tool to imitate the effect of spraying paint with an airbrush. The airbrush paints with the foreground colour.

| | To paint with the Airbrush tool, double-click the Airbrush tool to display the Airbrush Options palette if it is not already showing. Use the palette to specify the settings for: Blending Mode, Pressure and Fade. |

Use the Brushes palette to specify an Airbrush size and shape. Use a soft-edged brush to create the most realistic airbrush effect.

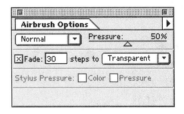

2 Click and drag across the image to apply the foreground colour. The more you spray over an area, the greater the build-up of colour. The speed at which you drag the airbrush also affects the intensity of the paint.

For a description of Blending modes see pages 76–77.

The Pencil Tool (Y)

You can use the Pencil tool to draw freeform lines. The lines you draw with the Pencil tool are always hard-edged – in other words, the edges of your lines are not anti-aliased. The Pencil tool paints or draws with the foreground colour.

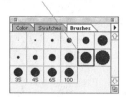

Use the Brushes palette to specify the size of your pencil.

| To draw a line, double-click the Pencil tool to show the Pencil Tool Options palette if it is not already showing. Use the Pencil Options palette to specify: Blending Mode, Opacity, Fade and Auto Erase options.

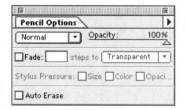

2 Click and drag to create a line. You can hold down the Shift key after you start drawing to create a straight line.

Auto Erase
Select this option to use the Pencil tool as an eraser.

The Gradient Tool (G)

You can use the Gradient tool to create transitions from one colour to another. You can also create multi-coloured gradients. Gradients can be linear or radial. You can apply a gradient fill to a selection, or to an entire, active layer.

1 To create a gradient fill, double-click the Gradient tool to show the Gradient Tool Options palette if it is not already showing.

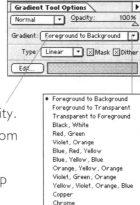

2 Select a Blending mode and set Opacity. Use the gradient pop-up to choose from one of the preset gradients. Choose Linear or Radial from the Type pop-up menu.

HANDY TIP

Hold down Shift as you click and drag to constrain a linear gradient to 45-degree increments.

3 Position your cursor where you want the gradient to start, then click and drag. The angle and distance you drag the cursor defines the angle and distance of a linear gradient, or the radius of a radial fill. (Click and drag from the centre out to create a radial fill.)

For a linear gradient, the start and end colours fill any part of the selection that you do not drag the cursor across. For radial gradients, the end colour fills the remaining area.

The Line Tool (N)

Use the Line tool to create straight lines. Lines are filled with the foreground colour. Lines are always hard-edged.

You cannot specify a brush size for the Line tool; use the Line Width setting in the Line Tool Options palette instead.

1 To draw a straight line, double-click the Line tool to show the Line Tool Options palette. Use the palette to specify Mode, Opacity and Line Width as desired.

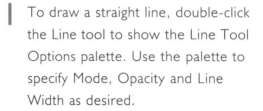

2 Click and drag on the image to create a line. You can hold down Shift as you click and drag to constrain the line to 45-degree increments.

You must specify arrowhead settings before you create a line.

3 To add arrowheads to the beginning or end of a line, click the Start/End options as appropriate. Click the Shape button to define the shape of the arrowhead.

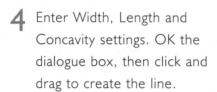

4 Enter Width, Length and Concavity settings. OK the dialogue box, then click and drag to create the line.

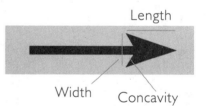

Length

Width   Concavity

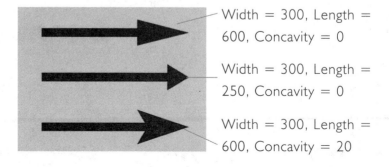

Width = 300, Length = 600, Concavity = 0

Width = 300, Length = 250, Concavity = 0

Width = 300, Length = 600, Concavity = 20

The Paint Bucket Tool (K)

You can use the Paint Bucket tool to colour pixels with the foreground colour, based on a tolerance setting. It works in a similar way to the Magic Wand tool, but in this case, filling adjoining pixels that fall within the tolerance setting. You can use the Paint Bucket tool without creating a selection.

1 To fill an area with the foreground colour, double-click the Paint Bucket tool to show the Paint Bucket Options palette if it is not already showing. Enter a value from 0–255 in the Tolerance box. The higher you set the value, the greater the range of pixels the Paint Bucket will fill.

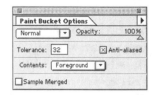

2 Set Opacity, Blending mode, Anti-aliased and Sample Merged options. Position your cursor then click on the image.

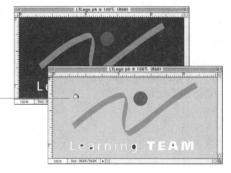

REMEMBER **The Anti-aliased option creates a slightly soft edge on the areas that the Paint Bucket fills.**

3 You can use the Paint Bucket to fill with a pattern previously saved into the pattern buffer. Use the contents pop-up to specify whether the Paint Bucket fills with the foreground colour or a pattern.

Blending Modes

REMEMBER

The blending modes allow you to make changes to an image using the painting and editing tools in a more selective and subtle way than simply painting with the foreground colour. The colour you paint with (the blend colour) combines with the colour of the pixels you drag across (the base colour) to produce a different colour depending on the blending mode you select.

REMEMBER

Blending modes are also available in the Layers palette and in the Fill Path, Fill, Stroke and Fade dialogue boxes.

| Normal |
| Dissolve |
| Behind |

| Multiply |
| Screen |
| Overlay |
| Soft Light |
| Hard Light |

| Color Dodge |
| Color Burn |

| Darken |
| Lighten |
| Difference |
| Exclusion |

| Hue |
| Saturation |
| Color |
| Luminosity |

Choose blending modes from the pop-up menu in the Painting Tool Options palettes. The various paint modes in combination with opacity/pressure settings have a selective control on which pixels are affected when you use the painting and editing tools.

As the name suggests, the result is more of a blending of the paint colour and the colour of the base pixels than simply one colour replacing another.

Dissolve
Produces a grainy, chalk-like effect. Not all pixels are coloured as you drag across the image, leaving gaps and holes in the stroke.

Behind
Only available when you are working on a layer with a transparent background. Use Behind to paint behind the existing pixels on a layer. Paint appears in the transparent areas, but does not affect the existing pixels.

Multiply
Combines the colour you are painting with the colour of the pixels you drag across, to produce a colour that is darker than the original colours.

Screen
Produces the opposite effect to Multiply. It multiplies the opposite of the original colour by the painting colour and has the effect of lightening the pixels.

Overlay
This increases the contrast and saturation, combining foreground colour with the pixels you drag across.

Soft Light
Creates a soft lighting effect. Lightens colours if the painting colour is lighter than 50% grey, darkens colours if the painting colour is darker than 50% grey.

...contd

Use the Opacity/ Pressure setting to control the intensity of the effect.

Be prepared to experiment with blending modes to fully understand their results and to get the best out of them.

Hard Light
Multiplies or screens pixels, depending on the paint colour, and tends to increase contrast.

Darken
Applies the paint colour to pixels that are lighter than the paint colour – doesn't change pixels darker than the paint colour.

Lighten
Replaces pixels darker than the paint colour, but does not change pixels lighter than the paint colour.

Difference
Results in inverting some pixels. It looks at the brightness of pixels and the paint colour, then subtracts paint brightness from pixel brightness. Depending on the result, it inverts the pixels.

Hue
Only works for colour images. Applies the hue (colour) of the paint, without affecting the saturation or luminosity of the pixels.

Saturation
Changes the saturation of pixels based on the saturation of the paint colour, but does not affect hue or luminosity.

Luminosity
Changes the relative lightness or darkness of the pixels without affecting their hue or saturation.

Colour
Applies the hue and saturation of the paint colour, but does not affect the luminosity of pixels.

Colour Dodge
Lightens the base colour – more pronounced when the paint colour is light.

Colour Burn
Darkens the base colour – more pronounced when paint colour is dark.

Defining a Brush

You can create your own custom brush strokes from selections.

1 To create a brushstroke, make
a selection, then choose Define
Brush from the pop-up menu in
the Brushes palette.
The new brush is
added to the Brushes
palette.

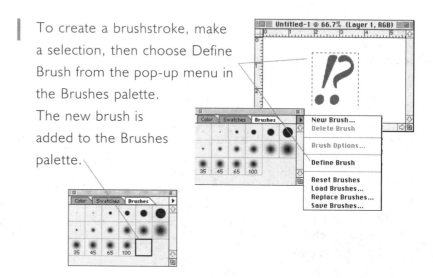

2 Double-click the brush if you
want to change the spacing and
anti-aliased options. Anti-aliased
is not available for very large
brush sizes.

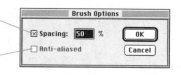

3 You can then use a painting tool to paint with the new
brush. In this example a fade of 30 has been set.

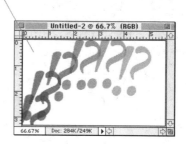

The Editing Tools

The editing tools – Eraser, Rubber Stamp, Smudge, Blur and Sharpen, Dodge, Burn, Saturate and Desaturate – allow you to edit or change pixels in a variety of ways.

The editing tools can be used within a selection or anywhere on an image. Use the Brushes palette to specify a brush size for the editing tool. Many of the techniques and keyboard shortcuts covered for the painting tools apply to the editing tools as well.

Covers

Chapter Seven

The Eraser Tool (E)

The Eraser tool is one of the editing tools. You can use it to erase portions of your image. The Eraser rubs out to the background colour when you are working on the background layer, and to transparency when you are working on any other layer.

 Use the Brushes palette to specify the Eraser size.

1 To erase areas of your image, double-click the Eraser tool to show the Eraser Options palette. Use the palette to specify Type, Opacity, Fade, Wet Edges and Erase to Saved options.

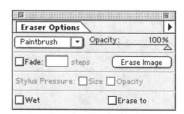

2 Click and drag on your image to erase to the background colour or transparency, depending on which layer you are working on.

 Hold down Alt/ Option (Mac) or Alt (Windows) with the Eraser tool selected to access the Erase to Saved option temporarily. Click and drag across modified areas of the image to restore them to the state they were at when you last saved the image.

Opacity
Use the opacity setting to create the effect of partially erasing pixels.

Mode
Use the Mode pop-up to choose an erase mode. The default is Paintbrush.

Erase Image
Click the Erase Image button to erase an entire layer to transparency, or to erase the background layer to the background colour.

Erase to Saved
Use this option to rub back portions of your image to their exact state when you last saved. When you position your cursor on the image, it changes shape; press and drag to restore modified pixels to their previous state.

The Smudge Tool (U)

You can use the Smudge tool to create an effect similar to dragging your finger through wet paint. The Smudge tool picks up colour from where you start to drag and smears it into adjacent colours.

1 Double-click the Smudge tool to show the Smudge Tool Options palette if it is not already showing. Set the pressure, position your cursor on the image, then start to drag across your image to smudge the colours. The higher the pressure setting, the more pronounced the effect.

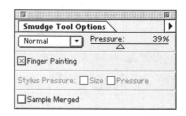

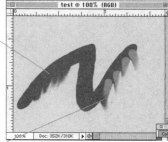

Hold down Alt/ Option (Mac) or Alt (Windows) to temporarily turn Finger Painting on or off depending on whether the option is selected in the Options palette.

2 Select the Finger Painting option if you want to begin the smudge with the foreground colour.

3 Select the Sample Merged option if you want to smudge colours from other layers in the image onto the layer you are working on. Leave this option deselected if you want the smudge to pick up colour from pixels on the active or target layer only.

Sample Merged
Select this option when you want Photoshop to take into account, or 'sample', pixels from layers other than the target layer. In other words, it samples from layers as if they were merged.

The Rubber Stamp Tool (S)

You can use the Rubber Stamp tool to retouch your image by cloning or duplicating areas of your image. This is very useful when you want to remove blemishes and scratches from images.

1 To clone an area of your image, double-click the Rubber Stamp tool to show the Rubber Stamp Options palette if it is not already showing. Remember to set an appropriate brush size.

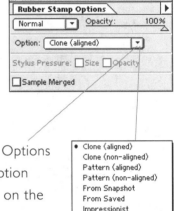

2 Select 'Clone (aligned)' from the Options pop-up menu. Hold down Alt/Option (Mac) or Alt (Windows) and click on the part of the image you want to clone.

3 Release Alt/Option or Alt. Move your cursor to a different part of your image, then click and drag. The pixels in the image where you drag are replaced by pixels cloned from the spot where you first clicked. A crosshair at the point where you first clicked indicates the pixels that are being cloned – the source point.

Clone (aligned)

The distance from the source point (represented by the crosshair) to the Rubber Stamp cursor remains fixed. This means that you can release the mouse, move the cursor, then continue to use the Rubber Stamp tool. The relative position of the source point and the Rubber Stamp cursor remain constant, but you will now be cloning pixels from a different part of the image.

...contd

Clone (non-aligned)

The source point – where you first click – remains the same. This means that if you stop dragging with the Rubber Stamp cursor, move to a different part of the image, then start dragging again, the pixels you clone continue to come from the original source point.

Pattern (aligned)

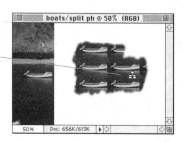

Use the Pattern (aligned) option with the Rubber Stamp tool to paint with a predefined pattern. Aligned means that even if you stop dragging and then restart, the pattern will align seamlessly.

HANDY TIP **To create a pattern, make a selection, then choose Edit > Define Pattern.**

Pattern (non-aligned)

This option paints with the predefined pattern, but does not align seamlessly if you stop dragging and then restart dragging.

Sample Merged

Select this option if you want to sample pixels from all layers when you define a source point. Leave this option deselected to sample pixels from the target layer only.

The Dodge, Burn and Sponge Tools (O)

The Dodge, Burn, Saturate/Desaturate group of tools are collectively called the 'Toning' tools. The Dodge and Burn tools are based on the traditional photographic technique of decreasing the amount of exposure given to a specific area on a print to lighten it (dodging), or increasing the exposure to darken areas (burning-in).

The Dodge Tool
Use the Dodge tool to lighten pixels in your image.

You cannot use the Dodge, Burn or Saturate/ Desaturate tools on a picture in bitmap or indexed colour mode.

1 To lighten areas of an image, select the Dodge tool. Remember to choose an appropriate brush size. A soft-edged brush usually creates the smoothest result. If the Toning Tools Options palette is not showing, you can double-click the Dodge tool to show it. Select Dodge from the Tools pop-up menu if you double-clicked on one of the other Toning tools.

It's a good idea to use a low exposure setting when you lighten areas of an image and build up the effect gradually.

2 Set the Midtone/Shadow/Highlight pop-up to limit changes to the middle range of greys, the dark or light areas of the image respectively, and also set Exposure.

3 Position your cursor on the image, then click and drag to lighten the pixels. Release the mouse then drag across the pixels again to intensify the effect.

...contd

The Burn Tool

Use the Burn tool to darken pixels in your image.

1 To darken areas of an image, select the Burn tool. Remember to choose an appropriate brush size. A soft-edged brush usually creates the smoothest result. If the Toning Tool Options palette is not showing, you can double-click the Burn tool to show it. Select Dodge from the Tools pop-up menu in the Toning Tools Options palette if you double-clicked on one of the other Toning tools.

2 Set the Midtone/Shadow/Highlight pop-up to limit changes to the middle range of greys, the dark or light areas of the image respectively, and also set Exposure.

3 Position your cursor on the image, then click and drag to lighten the pixels. Release the mouse then drag across the pixels again to intensify the effect.

In Greyscale Mode, the Sponge tool has the effect of increasing or decreasing contrast.

The Sponge Tool

You can use the Sponge tool when you want to subtly increase or decrease colour saturation in areas of your image.

1 To saturate/desaturate areas of an image, select the Sponge tool. Remember to select an appropriate brush size. If the Toning Tools Options palette is not showing, you can double-click the Sponge tool. Select Sponge from the Tools pop-up menu if you double-clicked on one of the other tools.

Each Toning tool retains its own settings when you switch to the other tools in the same group.

2 Set options for Saturate/Desaturate and Pressure.

3 Position your cursor on the image, then click and drag to alter the saturation.

The Blur and Sharpen Tools (R)

The Blur Tool

The Blur and Sharpen tools are the two 'Focus' tools. The Blur tool works by reducing contrast between pixels and can be useful for disguising unwanted, jagged edges and softening edges between shapes.

Remember to set an appropriate brush size before you start working with the Blur/Sharpen tool.

1 To blur areas of your image, select the Blur tool. If the Focus Tool Options palette is not showing, you can double-click the Blur tool to show it. Alternatively, select Blur from the Tools pop-up menu in the Options palette if you double-clicked on the Sharpen tool.

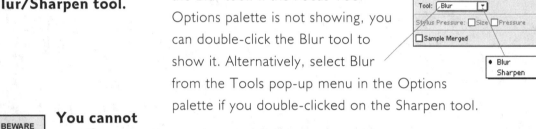

2 Set the Painting mode, Pressure and Sample Merged options, position your cursor on the image, then click and drag to blur the pixels. Release the mouse then drag across the pixels again to intensify the effect.

You cannot use the Blur/ Sharpen tool on an image in bitmap or indexed colour mode.

The Sharpen Tool

The Sharpen tool works by increasing the contrast between pixels.

1 To sharpen areas of an image, select the Sharpen tool. Double-click the Sharpen tool to show the Focus Tools Options palette. Alternatively, select Sharpen from the Tools pop-up menu in the Options palette if you double-clicked on the Blur tool.

Each Focus tool retains its own settings when you switch to the other tool.

2 Position your cursor, then click and drag to sharpen the pixels. Click and drag across the same area of the image again, to intensify the sharpening effect. You will produce a coarse, grainy effect if you overuse the Sharpen tool. Use a low pressure setting and build up the effect gradually.

Making Selections

One of the most important techniques when using Photoshop is making selections. When you make a selection, you are selecting an area of the image to which you want to make changes, and isolating the remainder of the image so that it is not affected by changes. A selection is indicated on-screen by a selection marquee – sometimes referred to as the 'marching ants' border.

Chapter Eight

Covers

The Marquee Selection Tool (M)

The Marquee selection tools allow you to drag with the mouse to make selections. You can make rectangular or elliptical selections by choosing the appropriate tool.

If you are working on an image with more than one layer, make sure you select the appropriate target layer before you make a selection.

1 To make a rectangular or oval selection, choose the Rectangular or Elliptical Marquee tool.

Hold down Shift, then click and drag with the Rectangular or Elliptical Marquee tool to create a square or circular selection. Hold down Alt/ Option (Mac) or Alt (Windows) to create a selection from the centre out.

2 Position your cursor on the image, then click and drag to define the area you want to select. When you release the cursor you will see a dotted rectangular or oval marquee defining the area of the selection.

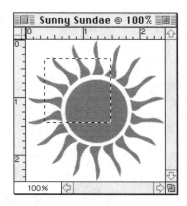

3 You can reposition the selection marquee if you need to. Make sure the Marquee tool is still selected, position your cursor inside the selection marquee (the cursor changes shape), then click and drag.

4 With the Marquee tool selected, you can deselect a selection by clicking inside or outside the selection marquee. Alternatively, you can choose Select > None.

As you are dragging to create a selection, you can hold down the spacebar to reposition the marquee.

Marquee Options

You can use the Marquee Options palette to make changes to the way in which the Marquee tools work.

| | Double-click the Marquee tool. The Marquee Options palette will appear if it is not already showing. Alternatively, select a Marquee tool, then choose Window > Show Options.

BEWARE

You can only have one selection active at a time, although a selection can consist of several non-contiguous areas.

2 You can use the Shape pop-up as an alternative to choosing a Selection tool using the toolbox.

3 Use the Style pop-up to create settings for making proportional selections, or selections of a fixed size.

REMEMBER

The Anti-aliased option is available in the Marquee, Lasso and Magic Wand Options palettes.

4 The Anti-aliased option is an important control when using bitmap applications such as Photoshop. Select anti-aliased to create a slightly blurred, soft edge around the selection and the pixels that surround the selection. Using Anti-aliased helps avoid creating unwanted jagged edges.

5 Use the Feather entry field to create a soft, feathered edge. (See pages 94–95 in this chapter.)

Moving Selections

You often need to move a selection (not the selection marquee) to a different position. You can do this using the Move tool.

1 Make a selection. Select the Move tool and then position your cursor inside the Marquee selection border. Click and drag to move the selection. Alternatively, with the Marquee or Lasso selection tool still selected, hold down Command (Mac) or Ctrl (Windows). The cursor changes to the Move tool cursor. Click and drag to move the selected pixels.

When you reposition a selection of pixels in this way they become a floating selection and appear as a temporary layer in the Layers palette.

Floating selections are useful and important. Whilst the floating selection is active, the pixels in the selection float above the underlying pixels, without replacing them.

HANDY TIP

To move the selection in increments of one pixel with the Move tool or a selection tool selected, press the up, down, left or right arrow keys. Hold down Shift and press the arrow keys to move the selection in increments of five pixels.

2 To 'defloat' the pixels so that they replace the underlying pixels, choose Select > None if you have the Move tool selected. If you used Command/Ctrl with a Marquee or Lasso tool selected, click outside the selection marquee. If you used Command/Ctrl with the Magic Wand tool selected, choose Select > None. The pixels that were underneath the floating selection – the underlying pixels – are now completely replaced by the pixels in the floating selection. The temporary floating selection disappears from the Layers palette.

...contd

3 Notice that the area that the pixels in the selection were moved from is filled with the currently selected background colour. (In a bitmap image, you cannot have an area where there are no pixels.)

4 To move a selection and make a copy of it at the same time, hold down Alt/Option (Mac) or Alt (Windows) before you drag with the Move tool. Alternatively, with a selection tool selected, hold down Command + Alt/Option (Mac), or Ctrl + Alt (Windows), then click and drag. The cursor turns into a double-headed arrow, indicating that you are copying the selection.

5 You can turn a floating selection into a layer by dragging the floating selection layer name onto the Create New Layer icon in the Layers palette.

You can also double-click the floating selection layer to show the Make Layer dialogue box.

6 Enter a name for the layer, then click OK. (See Chapter Nine for more information on layers.)

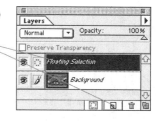

The Lasso Tool (L)

You can use the Lasso tool to make freeform selections by clicking and dragging. It is a useful tool for selecting irregular areas and for quickly adding to or subtracting from selections made with the Magic Wand tool.

1 Double-click the Lasso tool to show the Lasso Options palette if it is not already showing. Set Feather and Anti-aliased options.

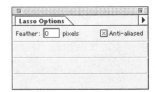

HANDY TIP

Hold down Shift, then click and drag around an area to add it to the selection. Hold down Command (Mac) or Ctrl (Windows), then click and drag around an area to remove it from the selection.

2 Position your cursor on the image. The cursor changes to the Lasso cursor.

3 Click and drag around the part of the image you want to select. Make sure your cursor comes back to the start point. If you release before reaching the start point, Photoshop completes the selection with a straight line. A dotted marquee defines the selected area.

BEWARE

If you have a feather amount set in the Lasso Options palette, you will not end up with straight lines.

4 Use the Polygon Lasso tool to create a freeform selection with straight line segments. Select the Polygon Lasso tool. Position your cursor on the image, then click; move the cursor, then click... and so on, until you have defined the area you want to select.

5 Click back at the start point to complete the selection. A small circle appears at the bottom right of the cursor to indicate the start. Alternatively, you can double-click to close the selection marquee.

The Magic Wand Tool (W)

The Magic Wand tool is useful for selecting continuous areas of colour in an image, based on a tolerance setting. A low tolerance setting will make a very limited selection of colour. A high setting will select a wider range of pixels. The tool is good for selecting consistently coloured areas, without having to trace the outline with the Lasso tool.

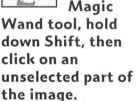

To add to a selection using the Magic Wand tool, hold down Shift, then click on an unselected part of the image.

1 Before you create a selection using the Magic Wand tool, check the tolerance setting. Double-click the Magic Wand tool to display the Magic Wand Options palette, or choose

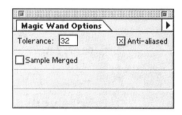

Window > Show Options to show the Tool Options palette, then select the Magic Wand tool. Enter a tolerance value from 0–255. If you set the maximum tolerance value of 255, you will select every pixel in the image.

2 Click on the image where you want to select pixels of similar colour value. All adjacent pixels that are within the tolerance range are selected. When you begin working with the Magic Wand tool, start off using the default setting of 32 and then adjust this as necessary to make the selection you require. Typically, you will use the Magic Wand in combination with the other selection tools and the Grow and Similar commands, which you use to fine-tune the initial Magic Wand selection.

You cannot use the Magic Wand tool in Bitmap mode.

3 To deselect a selection marquee when the Magic Wand tool is selected, click inside the selection marquee. If you click outside the selection marquee, you will create another selection based around the pixel where you clicked.

Feathering Selections

REMEMBER

You can define a feathered edge when you make selections using the Lasso tools and the Marquee tools.

You can use the Feather option to control the degree to which the edge of a selection is softened or faded. Feathering a selection creates a transition boundary between the selection and the surrounding pixels, which can cause a loss of detail.

BEWARE

Check the Options palette before you make a selection to make sure that there isn't a feather amount set if you don't want one.

1 Double-click one of the Lasso or the Marquee selection tools. The Options palette for the tool appears if it was not already showing.

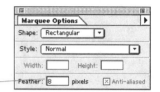

2 In the Options palette, set a feather value, e.g. 10. You can set a value from 1 to 250 pixels. The amount you set depends on the effect you want to achieve.

3 Create a selection using either the Marquee or Lasso tool. When you move the selection you will see the feathered edge around the selection and also where you move the selection from.

BEWARE

When you set a feather amount the selection you make may appear more 'rounded' than you expect. This is caused by the feather value.

4 Alternatively, you can make a selection and then choose Select > Feather. Enter a value for the Feather radius.

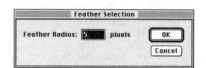

Creating a Vignette

You can use the feathering option to create a vignette effect – a soft, fading edge to an image.

1 Before you begin, make sure your background colour is set to white (see Chapter Five – Defining Colours). Then set a feather value in the Options palette for the selection tool you are using.

2 Next, create a selection, which can be a regular or irregular shape.

Feathering, unlike anti-aliasing, blurs the inside and outside of a selection boundary.

3 Choose Select > Inverse. This reverses the selection – selecting all the pixels that were previously not selected.

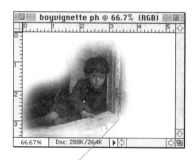

4 Press Delete (Mac) or Backspace (Windows) to delete the area surrounding your selection, leaving a feathered edge.

Colour Range Selections

The Colour Range selection dialogue provides another method for making complex selections based on colour values. Choose Select > Colour Range.

1 With the preview option set to Selection, and Sampled Colours as the Select option, set a fuzziness value. This determines how many shades of colour are selected. Low values limit the selection, higher values select a wider range of colours.

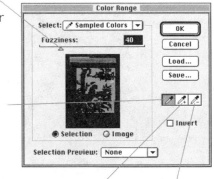

2 To select colours, click on the Eyedropper tool, then click in the main image window on the colour you want to select.

HANDY TIP

Use the Select pop-up to choose out-of-gamut colours. This selects those colours that will be automatically adjusted to fall within the CMYK gamut when you change mode from RGB to CMYK. Instead of letting Photoshop do this automatically, you can now use the Sponge tool, set to desaturate, to gradually bring the selected areas into gamut.

3 To add to the range of selected colours, select the Eyedropper Plus tool and click again in the image window, or in the Preview window within the dialogue box.

4 To subtract areas of colour from the selection, click the Eyedropper Minus tool, then click on a colour in the image or the Preview window that you want to subtract.

5 Experiment with the Selection preview to change the image window to indicate the colours selected. Different selection previews can help you make the selections you want.

6 OK the dialogue box to see the selection marquee around the selected range of colours.

Modifying Selections

There are many instances when you need to add to or subtract from a selection. You can use any combination of selection tools to make the selection you want. For example, you might start by making a selection with the Magic Wand tool, then add to the selection using the Lasso tool.

1 To add to an existing selection, hold down the Shift key, then click and drag to create another selection marquee that intersects the existing selection marquee.

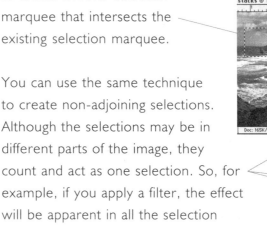

2 You can use the same technique to create non-adjoining selections. Although the selections may be in different parts of the image, they count and act as one selection. So, for example, if you apply a filter, the effect will be apparent in all the selection marquees.

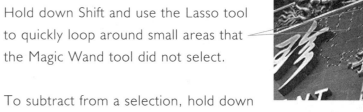

HANDY TIP **For complex selections, to see the selected pixels more clearly, it can be quite useful to hide the dotted selection border temporarily. Choose Select > Hide Edges to hide the selection border. The selection remains active; you have simply hidden the border. Choose Select > Show Edges to redisplay the selection border.**

3 Hold down Shift and use the Lasso tool to quickly loop around small areas that the Magic Wand tool did not select.

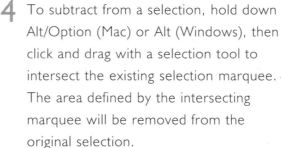

4 To subtract from a selection, hold down Alt/Option (Mac) or Alt (Windows), then click and drag with a selection tool to intersect the existing selection marquee. The area defined by the intersecting marquee will be removed from the original selection.

The Grow and Similar Commands

The Grow and Similar commands are very useful when used in conjunction with the Magic Wand tool to add to a selection. Both work according to the tolerance setting as set in the Magic Wand Options palette.

The Grow command selects contiguous or adjoining areas of colour based on the tolerance setting in the Magic Wand Options palette.

1   Make a selection. Check that the Tolerance setting in the Magic Wand Options palette is appropriate.

2   Choose Select > Grow. Pixels which fall within the Tolerance setting and are adjacent to pixels already in the selection are added to the selection.

The Similar command selects non-adjacent pixels that fall within the same tolerance setting as set in the Magic Wand Options palette.

1   Make a selection using any of the selection tools. Check that the Tolerance setting in the Magic Wand Options palette is appropriate.

2   Choose Select > Similar. Pixels throughout the image that fall within the Tolerance setting are selected.

Pasting Into Selections

Pasting into selections is a useful technique for compositing images.

1 Create a selection in the destination window.

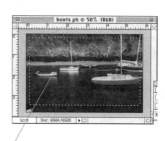

2 Open the source document, then make the selection you want to paste into the destination document. Choose Edit > Copy to copy the selection to the clipboard.

3 Click in the destination image window. The selection should still be active. Choose Edit > Paste Into to paste the clipboard selection into the selected area.

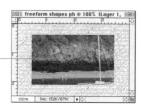

4 Use the Move tool to reposition the pasted selection relative to the original selection.

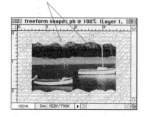

5 The Paste Into command has created a layer mask. The layer is active, indicated by the paintbrush icon in the Layers palette, which means that you can edit the layer. To edit the mask, click the mask icon in the Layers palette. A small circle replaces the paintbrush, indicating that the layer mask is selected.

The Defringe Command

You can drag a selection from one window to another image window. This is useful when creating a composite image. Defringe is useful when you use this technique, as it helps to blend the selection into its new environment.

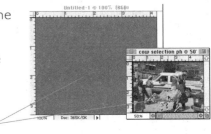

1   To drag a selection from one image window to another, first make a selection in the source window. Select the Move tool, position the Move cursor inside the selection, then click and drag into the destination window.

2   When you release the mouse button, the selection appears in the destination window on a new layer. The destination window becomes the active window, and the new layer is the active layer. Check to see if there are unwanted pixels causing a halo effect around the edge of the selection.

HANDY TIP

A width setting of 1 or 2 pixels is usually sufficient to defringe a pasted or moved selection.

3   To defringe the moved selection, make sure the newly created layer is active, and make sure Preserve Transparency is deselected. Choose Layer > Matting > Defringe. Enter a value for the width, then OK the dialogue box. The selection should now blend in better.

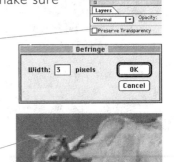

Filling a Selection

You can use the Fill dialogue box to fill an entire layer or a selection.

1 To fill a selection, first define either a foreground or background colour that you want to fill with, then make a selection. Choose Edit > Fill. Use the Contents pop-up to choose the fill type. You can also set Opacity for the fill and a blending mode. OK the dialogue box.

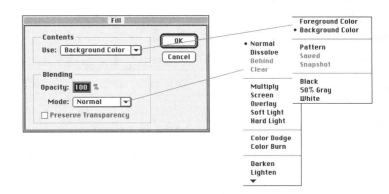

See pages 76–77 for a description of the blending modes.

2 To fill a selection with a pattern, first define the pattern by making a selection, then choosing Edit > Define Pattern.

3 Choose Edit > Fill. Choose Pattern from the Contents pop-up. OK the dialogue box to fill the selection with the pattern.

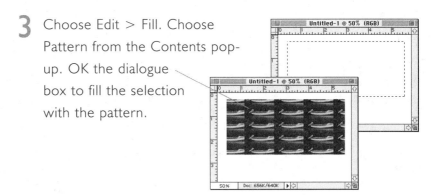

Transforming Selections

Sometimes you need to manipulate a selection, to make it bigger, rotate it, or skew it. You can do this using the Free Transform option in the Layer menu.

The advantage of Free Transform is that you can make multiple transformations, then either accept the result or not.

1 Make a selection, then Choose Layer > Free Transform. A transform marquee appears around the selection. Drag handles to resize the selection. To resize in proportion, hold down Shift, then click and drag a corner handle.

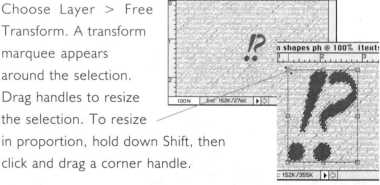

2 To rotate the selection, position the cursor just outside the transform marquee, then click and drag in a circular direction.

When you transform a selection in this way it temporarily becomes a floating selection.

3 To skew the selection, hold down Command (Mac) or Ctrl (Windows) and Shift, then click and drag a side handle.

4 To reposition the transform selection, position your cursor inside the transform border, then click and drag.

5 To reposition corner handles independently, hold down Command (Mac) or Ctrl (Windows), then click and drag a corner handle. Hold down Shift as you do so to constrain the effect. You can set up perspective effects using this technique.

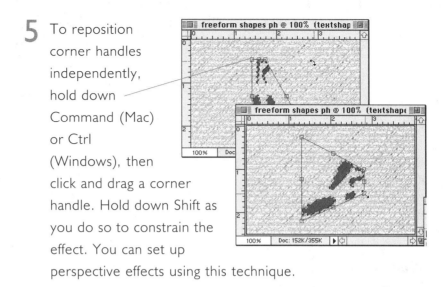

6 To accept the transformations and remove the transform marquee, press Return/Enter, or double-click inside the transform marquee.

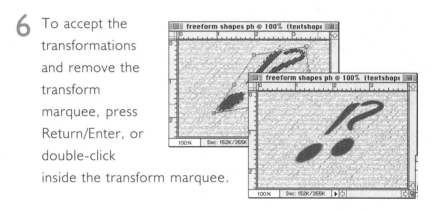

7 To revert to the original selection without making changes, press the Esc key.

Copying and Pasting Selections

You can use the clipboard to copy and past selections within the same image and into other images.

A useful technique for selecting a simple image, like the runner on this page, is the Inverse selection command. Use the Magic Wand tool to select the background, then choose Select > Inverse to reverse the selection. The areas that make up the image are now selected.

I To copy a selection, first make a selection using any of the selection tools. Choose Edit > Copy.

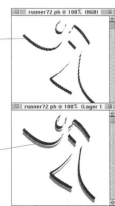

2 To paste the selection into the same image, choose Edit > Paste. The selection is pasted into the image on its own layer. (For information on working with layers, see Chapter Nine, 'Layers'.)

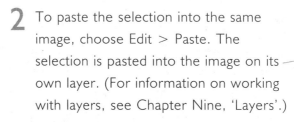

3 To paste the selection into another image, click on the other image window if it is already open, or use File > Open to open another image. Choose Edit > Paste to paste the selection from the clipboard onto a new layer in the active image.

4 You can also drag a selection from one image window into another. You need two images open – the source and the destination windows. Make a selection in the source window, select the Move tool, position your cursor within the selection, then click and drag into the destination window. The selection appears on its own layer.

Use the Defringe command (see page 100) to help a pasted or dragged selection blend into its new surroundings.

Layers

Layers introduce a considerable degree of flexibility into the way in which you can work in Photoshop. Layers allow you to keep various elements of your image separate so that you can make changes without deleting or changing the underlying pixels in the image. You can add, delete and restack layers.

Each additional layer that you create increases the file size of the image. When you have finished editing your image, you can selectively merge layers into each other. You will need to do this to use your image in QuarkXPress or Adobe PageMaker. You should note that you can only save images with layers in Photoshop format.

When you create or open an image for the first time, it consists of one default layer called Background.

Covers

Chapter Nine

Working with Layers

To access the Layers palette, choose Window > Show
Layers.

**New layers
are auto-
matically
created
when you use the
Type tool to add
text to an image,
when you drag or
copy a selection
into an image, and
also when you drag
a layer from one
document into
another.**

1 To create a new layer, either click
once on the New Layer icon at the
bottom of the Layers palette, or
use the pop-up menu in the Layers
palette and choose New Layer.

2 Enter a name for the
layer in the New
Layer dialogue box.
You can also choose
opacity and blending
mode settings at this stage if you want to.

3 OK the dialogue box, or press Return/Enter. The new layer
appears in the Layers palette above the previously
highlighted layer. Notice also that the file size in the
Document Sizes status bar area increases when you paint on
the layer or add pixels to the layer.

**To edit
Layer
Options
for a
Layer, double-click
the layer name. The
Layer Options
dialogue box
appears. Make
changes as
necessary, then OK
the dialogue box.**

4 To delete a layer, click on the layer to
select it. Then choose Delete Layer from
the pop-up menu in the Layers palette.
Alternatively, drag the Layer name onto the
Wastebasket icon at the
bottom of the Layers
palette. Click Yes or No in
the Delete Layer warning
box.

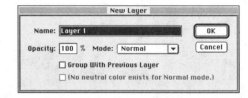

...contd

Selecting, Hiding and Showing Layers

You can only work on one layer at a time. This is often referred to as the 'target' layer.

1 Click on the layer name in the Layers palette to make it active. The layer name will highlight and the paintbrush icon will appear in the second column on the left of the palette.

You can nudge the contents of a selected layer in 1-pixel increments by pressing the arrow keys when the Move tool is selected.

2 To hide a layer, click on the eye icon in the leftmost column of the Layers palette. To show a layer, click in the leftmost column to bring back the eye icon.

Reordering Layers

It is often necessary to reorder the stacking position of layers, in order to control which layers appear in front of other layers.

You can move pixels in a layer beyond the edge of your picture. These non-visible pixels will be saved with the document, but they will be deleted when you use any editing tool to modify pixels, or if you use any image-editing command. These non-visible pixels will be lost when you flatten or merge layers in an image.

1 To change the layering order, click and drag the layer name you want to reposition. Notice the black horizontal bar that appears as you move the layer upwards or downwards. Release the mouse when the black bar appears in the position to which you want the layer moved.

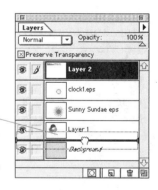

Repositioning Layers

You can reposition the entire contents of a layer using the Move tool.

Click on the layer you want to move in the Layers palette. Select the Move tool, then position your cursor anywhere on the image. Click and drag to move the layer.

Floating Selections and Layers

You create floating selections in Photoshop when you use the Move tool to move a selection.

A floating selection will automatically appear in the Layers palette above the currently active layer as a temporary layer called 'Floating Selection'. A dotted marquee icon also appears in the column next to the eye icon.

If you defloat (Layers > Defloat) or deselect (Select > None) a floating selection, it will replace the underlying pixels on the layer below it. To prevent this from happening, you can turn the floating selection into a layer.

REMEMBER

Hold down Alt/ Option (Mac) or Alt (Windows) then click and drag with the Move tool to make a copy of a selection. (See pages 76–77 for a description of the blending modes.)

1 To turn a floating selection into a layer, create a floating selection, then double-click the temporary floating selection layer name. Alternatively, you can drag the floating selection layer onto the New Layer icon at the bottom of the Layers palette.

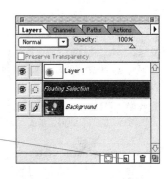

2 Enter a name for the layer in the Make Layer dialogue box. You can also choose opacity and blending mode settings at this stage if you want to.

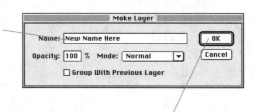

3 OK the dialogue box, or press Return/Enter. The new layer appears in the Layers palette.

Merging and Flattening Layers

The Merge Visible Layers command in the pop-up menu merges only the currently visible layers.

Use the Merge commands to combine two or more layers into one layer. This is useful for keeping file size down and for consolidating elements on different layers into a single manageable layer or unit.

1 To merge all the visible layers in your document, first hide any layers you don't want to merge, make sure one of the layers you want to merge is active, then choose Merge Visible from the pop-up menu in the Layers palette, or choose Layer > Merge Visible.

When you use the Flatten Image command, any hidden layers will be discarded.

2 To merge a layer with the layer below it, first select the layer, then choose Merge Down from the pop-up menu, or choose Layer > Merge Down.

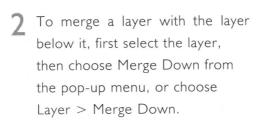

When you convert images between some modes you are prompted to flatten the file. Make sure you save a copy of the file first if you want to be able to go back and do further work on the layers.

Flattening Images

When you flatten an image, you end up with a background layer only. This reduces the file size. Flatten an image when you have finished creating and positioning the elements of your composite image, and are ready to save the file in a suitable format for placing in a page layout application.

1 To flatten an image, make sure that all the layers you want to keep are visible. Choose Flatten Image from the Layers palette pop-up menu, or choose Layers > Flatten Image.

Moving Layers Between Images

You can copy a complete layer from one Photoshop document to another; you can also move a selection from one document to another.

BEWARE

The layer you move into a different image window is rendered at the resolution of the destination window. This causes the elements on the moved layer to appear larger or smaller than in the original window. Also, if the modes of the two images are different, the layer you move will be converted to match the mode of the destination window.

1 First make sure you have two document windows open – a 'source' document and a 'destination' document. The source document contains the layer you want to copy. The destination document is the document into which you want to copy the layer.

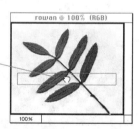

2 Click in the source document window to make it active. Position your cursor on the layer in the Layers palette, then drag the layer you want to copy from the source document into the destination document window. You will see a bounding box indicating the layer you are copying.

REMEMBER

Use the Defringe command (see page 100) to remove any fringe around pixels on a layer that you copy from one image to another.

3 Position the layer and then release the mouse. The layer becomes the topmost layer in the Layers palette of the destination document. The destination document is now the active image window.

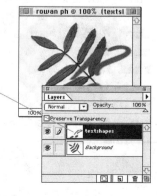

Linking Layers

Linking layers is useful when you want to keep elements of an image on separate layers, but you need to move the layers maintaining the exact positional relationship of each.

1. To move the foreground object with its shadow (which is on a separate layer), show the Layers palette (Window > Show Layers) and make sure that one of the layers you want to link is active.

2. Click in the empty box to the right of the eye icon of the layer you want to link. A chain icon appears in the box, indicating that the layer is linked. When you make the linked layer active, the chain and paintbrush icons switch to indicate the layer you are working on.

3. Use the Move tool to reposition the elements on the linked layers as one.

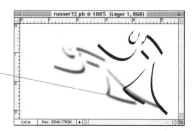

4. You can link multiple layers using the same technique.

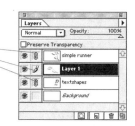

5. To unlink a layer, click the chain icon. The layer is now completely independent again.

Adjustment Layers

Using an adjustment layer is like positioning a lens above the pixels on the layers below it to change their appearance. If you don't like the result, you can edit the adjustment layer to achieve the result you want, or you can discard the adjustment layer. When you are satisfied with the result you can implement the adjustment layer as a permanent change.

An adjustment layer is created above the currently active layer. Its settings are applied to the layers below it and do not affect layers above.

1 Select a layer in the Layers palette. The adjustment layer will be positioned above the currently active layer. From the Layers palette pop-up choose New Adjustment Layer, or choose Layer > New > Adjustment.

You can restack adjustment layers as any other layer.

2 Choose a type from the Type pop-up menu. This automatically becomes the name for the layer. Enter a different name if desired. Set opacity and blending mode at this stage if you want to. Click OK.

3 Depending on the type of adjustment layer you chose, the appropriate dialogue box opens. Create the settings you want to experiment with. OK the dialogue box.

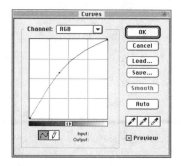

...contd

4 The new adjustment layer appears in the Layers palette as the active layer. The settings you created are now applied to all layers below the adjustment layer.

5 Click the eye icon to hide/show the preview of the changes brought about by the adjustment layer settings. Double-click the adjustment layer to re-enter the appropriate adjustment dialogue box to make changes to the settings.

REMEMBER

The adjustment layer settings do not have a permanent effect on pixels until the layer is merged with other layers, or the image is flattened.

6 Drag the adjustment layer into the wastebasket if you want to discard the settings.

7 When you are ready to make the settings of the adjustment layer permanent, either use one of the Merge commands from the pop-up, or flatten the image.

Transparency

Layers have transparent areas where there are no pixels on the layer, allowing you to see through to pixels on other layers. Preserve Transparency enables you to control which pixels are affected when you paint on or edit a layer.

HANDY TIP

Hold down Alt/ Option (Mac) or Alt (Windows) and click an eye icon to hide all other layers. Hold down Alt/ Option (Mac) or Alt (Windows) and click the eye icon again to show all layers.

1 To see transparent areas of a layer, hide all other layers by clicking on their eye icons. The transparent areas of the layer are represented by the checkerboard.

2 To work on a layer without affecting any of the transparent areas, select a layer, then make sure you select the Preserve Transparency option. In this example, painting with the Airbrush tool colours only existing pixels and does not affect the transparent areas of the layer where there are no pixels.

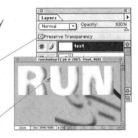

3 To colour existing pixels and the currently transparent areas of a layer, click the Preserve Transparency option to switch it off. Now when you paint on the layer or edit it in other ways, the transparent areas can be coloured – they are no longer protected from changes you make.

HANDY TIP

To select all pixels on a layer, hold down Command/Ctrl and click on the layer name in the Layers palette.

4 You can make pixels on individual layers semi-transparent by changing the opacity setting for the layer.

Working with Type

Type in Photoshop is made up of pixels, exactly the same as any other pixels in the image. This can make type harder to work with than type in applications such as QuarkXPress and Adobe Illustrator. For example, once you have created type it can be difficult to kern character pairs or correct spelling – it is best to get this sort of detail correct before you OK the Type Tool dialogue box.

Once you merge type with any other layer it becomes harder to select it and manipulate it further. Despite this, type in Photoshop is enormously flexible and versatile. You can choose different alignments vertically and horizontally for type, you can rotate it, fill it with a gradient, pattern or image, create translucent type and much more.

Covers

Chapter Ten

Creating Type

When you create type, it is automatically placed on its own layer. It is advisable to keep type on a separate layer, make all modifications and changes as necessary, and only when you are certain that you have done everything you need to do, merge it with other layers.

When you create type in Adobe Photoshop, it is created at the same resolution as the image itself. The foreground colour is automatically applied to the type you create.

1 To create type, select the Type tool, position your cursor on the image and click. This positions the start point of your type. The Type Tool dialogue box will appear.

The first time you use the Type tool you will have to wait a few seconds whilst Photoshop builds its font list.

2 Create settings for Font, Size, Leading, Spacing, Style and Alignment, then click into the text entry window at the bottom of the dialogue box and type in the

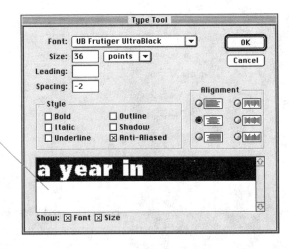

text you want. Press Return (Mac) or Enter (Windows) to start a new line, otherwise the type will appear on one line.

3 Click OK or press Enter on the numeric keypad to place the type on a new layer in the image.

Font

Use the Font pop-up menu to choose from the font list.

Size

Enter a value in the Size box for the size of your type. Use the Size pop-up menu to choose either points or pixels.

Leading

Leading controls the distance from one baseline of type to the next. Enter a leading value in the leading entry box. Leading is measured according to the size

And the nights that have come between

measurement option (points or pixels) that is selected. Photoshop applies a default leading value of 125% of the type size you have selected if you leave the leading box empty.

Spacing

You can set values for tracking/range kerning using the spacing option. Enter values from -99.9 to 999.9.

Negative values reduce the space, positive values increase the space. Again, the unit of measurement selected in the Size pop-up determines the distance characters move.

And   the   Spacing = 5 (16 pt text)

And the   Spacing = -2 (16 pt text)

If you apply bold style to a font such as ß Frutiger Bold, you will embolden the already bold font. If you apply italic to I Times Italic, you will end up with an italic that is further (machine) slanted. If you apply bold or italic to a Roman or plain font, Photoshop will use the true bold or italic font as long as it is available on the system.

Style

You can select one or more style options to apply to your text. Anti-aliased is selected by default.

Anti-aliased

The anti-aliased option creates type with a slightly soft edge. It does this by blurring the pixels that form the edge of the type. Use this option to avoid unnecessary jagged edges in type, unless you are working with very small type.

Anti-aliased text has a softer edge, which is usually desirable. Text that is not anti-aliased can look jagged. The text opposite has been scaled to 200% to make the difference more prominent.

Alignment

Select an adjustment option to specify how type aligns relative to the point at which you clicked using the Type tool.

There are three options for creating vertically aligned text.

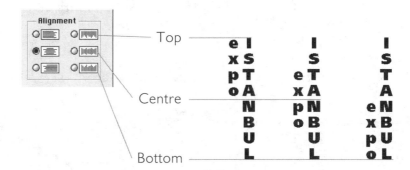

Show Font/Size

Use the Show Font/Size check boxes to control the way you view text you enter in the text entry window.

Deselecting the size option is useful when you specify large point sizes, but want to read and edit the text easily.

Filling and Repositioning Type

As long as your type is on its own layer, you can use the following procedure to change its colour.

1 First make sure that either the foreground or background colour is set to the colour you want your type to be. Make sure that the Preserve Transparency option is selected. Preserve Transparency means that when you use the Fill

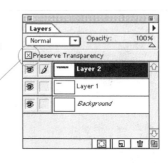

command in the next step, only pixels that already have a colour applied to them will be changed. The 'transparent' areas – that is, areas that do not already contain pixels – will not be affected.

BEWARE

If you reposition type so that parts of it are not visible on the canvas, the pixels which do not fit in the canvas area will be saved when you save the file, but as soon as you merge layers or perform any editing they will be discarded.

2 Choose Edit > Fill. Choose either background or foreground colour from the Use pop-up menu. Leave Opacity at 100%, then click OK. The type is filled accordingly.

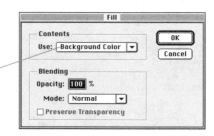

Repositioning Type

With type on its own layer, it is an easy matter to reposition it. You can even reposition the type so that parts of it are not visible.

To move type that is on its own layer, make sure the layer is active, select the Move tool, position your cursor in the image window, then click and drag.

Pasting into Type

You can achieve visually interesting results by pasting an image inside a type selection.

1 Open an image which contains the elements you want to paste into your type selection.

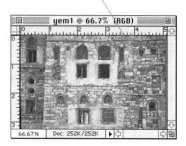 

2 Choose File > New to create a new image window. Enter the dimensions and resolution. If you want the new window to have the same settings as the image already open, use the Window menu and choose the appropriate file from the bottom of the menu. The new dialogue box is updated with the existing settings from the image you selected. OK the dialogue box.

3 Select the Type Mask tool. Position your cursor, then click. Create settings for type and enter the text you want to paste an image into. OK the dialogue box.

4 Keep the Type Mask tool selected. Position your cursor inside the outlined type selection and drag the type to reposition it if necessary. Be careful not to deselect the type selection.

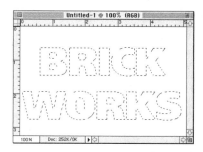

...contd

5 Click in the image window you previously opened. Make a suitable size selection, or choose Select > All. Use Edit > Copy to copy the selected pixels to the clipboard.

6 Click in the text window to make it active. Choose Edit > Paste Into to paste the contents of the clipboard into the type selection. This now becomes a layer mask. Use the Move tool to reposition the contents within the type outline.

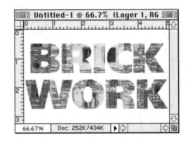

HANDY TIP

See pages 144–145 for information on layer masks. See page 109 for details on merging and flattening layers.

7 When you are satisfied, flatten the image and save.

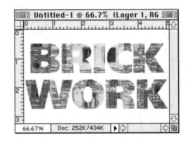

Type with a Soft Shadow

Another subtle, extremely effective type effect is to create a soft drop shadow.

1 In this example, make sure that the default foreground and background colours are selected, then use the Switch icon to make white the foreground colour.

2 Create some text. When you OK the Type Tool dialogue box, the type appears on a new layer filled with the foreground colour. If it is the wrong size or there is any other mistake, simply drag the new layer down onto the Wastebasket icon to delete it, then start again.

3 Use the Layer menu, or the pop-up menu in the Layers palette, and choose Duplicate Layer. Enter a name in the Duplicate Layer box, then click OK. You get an exact replica of your type sitting exactly on top of the original. This will form the headline and the type on Layer 1 will become the soft shadow.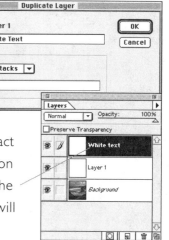

4 Click on Layer 1 to make it the active layer. Make sure Preserve Transparency is selected. Choose Edit > Fill. In the fill dialogue box choose Background Colour from the Use pop-up. Leave Opacity at 100%. OK the dialogue box.

5 Use the Move tool to reposition the black text to form a drop shadow. When you start to move the layer, you see the result of filling with background colour in previous step. Or, with the Move tool selected, you can press the arrow keys to move the layer in 1-pixel increments. You now have a hard-edged drop shadow.

6 Still working on Layer 1, this time make sure that Preserve transparency is deselected, so that when we apply a Gaussian Blur to the black text in the next step, the effect can spread into areas of the layer that are currently transparent.

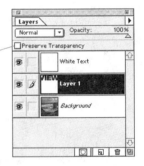

7 Choose Filter > Blur > Gaussian Blur. Enter a value of roughly 4, depending on the effect you want to achieve. OK the dialogue box. You now have a soft shadow on the white text.

Paths

An understanding of paths in Photoshop is essential for creating cut-outs for use in page layout applications such as QuarkXPress and Adobe PageMaker.

You can save paths with the image file in Photoshop format, convert paths into selections, or convert selections into paths. You can also export paths to Adobe Illustrator.

Covers

Chapter Eleven

Converting Selections to Paths

A quick, easy technique for creating a path is to make a selection, convert the selection into a work path, and then into a path.

Use Window > Show Paths to show the Paths palette.

1 First make a selection using any of the selection tools. Then, use the Paths palette pop-up menu and choose Make Work Path, or click the Make Work Path icon.

You can only have one work path in the Paths palette at any one time. A work path is a temporary path only. For a path to be saved when you save your file, you must first save the path (see step 4).

2 The Make Work Path dialogue box appears if you use the Make Work Path command. Specify a tolerance value (from 0.5– 10). (If you click the icon, the last-used settings from the dialogue box are applied automatically.) The tolerance value controls how closely the path conforms to the selection. A low tolerance value creates a path that follows the selection tightly. A high tolerance value produces a path that follows the selection more loosely.

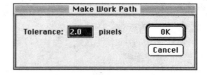

3 OK the dialogue box. A work path appears in the Paths palette, along with a thumbnail of the path.

4 Choose Save Path from the pop-up menu if you want to save this path before

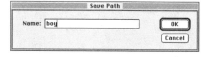

making any adjustments to it. Enter a name. OK the dialogue box. The new path appears in the palette, replacing the work path.

5 To hide the path, click in empty space in the Paths palette, or choose Turn Off Path from the pop-up menu. To show the path, click on the path name to select it. The path is highlighted.

New Path...
Duplicate Path...
Delete Path
Turn Off Path

Make Work Path...

Make Selection...
Fill Path...
Stroke Path...

Clipping Path...

Palette Options...

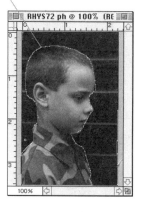

HANDY TIP

Click in an empty area of the Paths palette to turn off the path, leaving the selection marquee only visible in the image window.

Converting Paths to Selections

You can also convert a path into a selection. This is useful when you want a very accurate selection.

To convert a path into a selection, click on the path in the Paths palette to highlight it. Then choose Make Selection from the pop-up menu, or click the Make Selection icon.

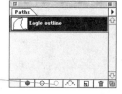

Creating Paths Using the Pen Tool

You can use the Pen tool to create paths. When you start to create a path it appears as a 'work path' in the Paths palette. A work path is only a temporary path.

The Pen tool creates anchor points which are connected by straight lines or curved segments. You can use the other tools in the Paths tool group to modify a path by adding, deleting or moving anchor points, and by changing the nature of the point, from smooth to corner and vice versa. You can also edit curved segments by dragging the Bezier direction points.

1   To create a path, double-click the Pen tool in the Toolbox to display the Pen Tool Options palette if it is not already showing. You can select the Rubber band option if you want to see a preview of the line segments as you draw.

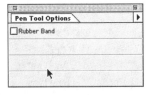

2   Position your cursor where you want to start drawing the path, then click, release the button, move the mouse and click again to create a straight line segment. Continue moving your cursor and clicking to create further straight line segments.

HANDY TIP

You can press the Delete key to delete the last anchor point. If you press Delete twice, you will delete the entire path.

...contd

3 Alternatively, you can click and drag to set an anchor point and create direction lines for a curve segment.

4 Then, release the button and move the cursor, and again click and drag to create the next anchor point with direction lines.

5 Continue in this way to create the path you want.

 You can only have one work path in a file. It is a good idea to save the path and give it a name, so you do not delete it accidentally by creating another work path. See pages 126–127 for details on saving your work path.

6 Position the Pen tool cursor at the start point. Notice the cursor now has a small circle attached to it. Click to create a closed path. The path will appear in the Paths palette with the default title of Work Path.

7 To create an open path, follow the techniques outlined above, but instead of clicking back at the start point, click on the Pen tool in the Toolbox to finish the path. This is now an open path to which you could, for example, apply a stroke.

Showing and Selecting Paths and Points

Use the following techniques for selecting, deselecting and deleting paths.

1 To select a path, first you have to show it. To do this, click the path name in the Paths palette. The path now shows in the image window.

2 To select the path, select the Direct Selection tool (the hollow arrow). If necessary, click on the path to make it active. You will now see the curve and line segments together with the anchor points.

3 Click on the anchor point of a curve segment to select the point and display the direction points.

4 To select and move an entire path, follow step 1 above, then hold down Alt/Option (Mac) or Alt (Windows) and click on the path. Using the Direct Selection tool, position your cursor on an anchor point or curve segment, then click and drag to reposition the path. To deselect a path, click away from the path using the Direct Selection tool.

5 To delete a path, with a point or line segment of the path selected, press the Delete key twice. Alternatively, with the entire path selected, press the Delete key once. You can also drag the path name onto the Wastebasket icon in the Paths palette.

Adding, Deleting and Converting Points

You often need to add points and delete points on a path.

1 To add a point to a path, make sure the path is selected, select the Add Point tool from the Pen group of tools, position your cursor on the path and then click. If you click on a curve segment you automatically get an anchor point with direction points. If you click on a straight line segment, you get just an anchor point.

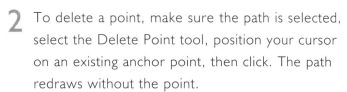

For a smooth point, when you drag one of the direction points, the other point balances it to maintain a smooth curve at the anchor point.

2 To delete a point, make sure the path is selected, select the Delete Point tool, position your cursor on an existing anchor point, then click. The path redraws without the point.

3 To convert a smooth point into a corner point, select the Convert Anchor Point tool, position your cursor on a direction point, then click and drag. Use the Direct Selection tool to make any further changes to the direction points.

A corner point is one which allows a sharp change of direction at the anchor point. Notice that for a corner point, when you drag one of the direction points, the other point is not affected. You have complete, independent control over each direction point.

4 To convert anchor points on straight line segments into smooth points, select the Convert Anchor Point tool, position your cursor on the anchor point, then click and drag. Direction lines appear around the point. Use the Direct Selection tool to make any further changes to the points.

5 To convert a smooth point into a corner point without direction lines, select the Convert Anchor Point tool, then click on an anchor point.

Creating Corner Points

As you use the Pen tool to create paths, you can draw corner points as you go, in combination with straight line segments and smooth points. In many instances, a smooth point cannot create the shape of the path you want.

A corner point allows a sharp change of direction at the anchor point. In a corner point, the direction points can be manipulated independently. This is what makes them essential to create paths that require sharp changes of direction.

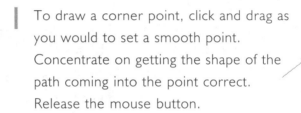

BEWARE

The paths in these screen shots have been moved one pixel away from the edge of the leaf so that they display more clearly. When you create a clipping path, it is best to position the path a pixel or so inside the shape you want to cut out, to avoid unwanted edge pixels being included. Unwanted edge pixels are sometimes referred to as 'edge tear'.

1 To draw a corner point, click and drag as you would to set a smooth point. Concentrate on getting the shape of the path coming into the point correct. Release the mouse button.

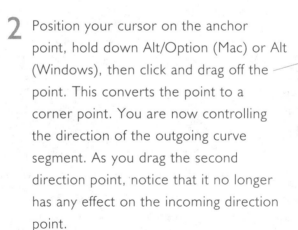

2 Position your cursor on the anchor point, hold down Alt/Option (Mac) or Alt (Windows), then click and drag off the point. This converts the point to a corner point. You are now controlling the direction of the outgoing curve segment. As you drag the second direction point, notice that it no longer has any effect on the incoming direction point.

3 Move your cursor, then continue drawing either smooth or corner points.

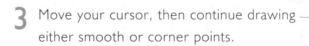

Editing Points

Paths invariably need to be modified and fine-tuned to produce the result you require.

Select the Direct Selection tool to edit paths and points (see page 130, 'Showing and Selecting Paths and Points').

Select an anchor point and press the arrow keys to move the selected point in 1-pixel increments.

1 To edit a smooth point, make sure the path is selected, then click on the anchor point to select it. Direction points appear either side of the anchor point. Direction points control the shape and length of a curve segment.

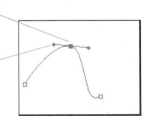

2 When you drag a direction point of a smooth anchor point, as you change the angle of one side, the other direction point moves to balance the point you are moving. This ensures the curve is always smooth through the anchor point.

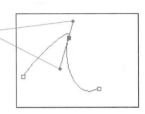

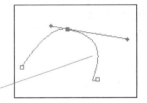

3 The further away from the anchor point you drag a direction point, the longer the associated curve segment becomes. As the curve segment is anchored at the anchor points at either end, this causes the curve segment to bow out more. Bring the direction point closer to the anchor point and the curve segment becomes shorter.

4 When you drag direction points on a corner anchor point, each moves totally independently of the other, allowing a sharp change of direction at the point.

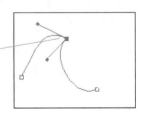

Exporting Clipping Paths

Create a clipping path when you want to create transparent areas in an image that you intend to use in an application such as Adobe Illustrator or QuarkXPress.

A clipping path makes areas of the image outside the path transparent, allowing you to see past the outline of the image to the background.

Flatness allows a PostScript printer to create less memory-intensive paths at output. If you use too high a flatness value, you get an approximate path that does not accurately conform to the path you created.

Flatness allows a PostScript printer to create less memory-intensive paths at output. If you use too high a flatness value, you get an approximate path that does not accurately conform to the path you created.

For high-resolution printing (1200–2400 dpi) a flatness value of 8 to 10 is generally recommended. Use a value of 1 to 3 for low resolution printing (300–600 dpi). Leave the field blank to use the printer's default setting.

| Create a saved path (see page 126). If you have more than one path in the Paths palette, make sure you select the appropriate path. Use the pop-up palette to select Clipping Path.

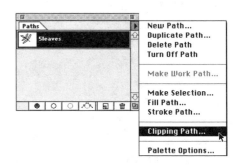

2 Use the Path pop-up to specify a different path to make into a clipping path if necessary. Enter a flatness value.

3 Choose File > Save As. In the Save As dialogue box, give the file a name and specify where you want to save it.

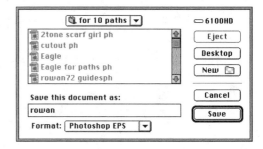

...contd

Remember to convert the file to an appropriate mode – e.g. CMYK – before you save the file in EPS format.

Select a TIFF preview option if you intend to use the image on the Windows platform.

4 Choose Photoshop EPS from the Format pop-up. Click Save.

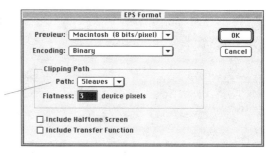

5 In the EPS Format dialogue box, specify a path that you want to be exported with the file as a clipping path. (You may have more than one clipping path in an image, but you can only export one clipping path per file.) Set Preview and Encoding options (see page 42 in Chapter Three). OK the dialogue box.

6 When you import the file into a QuarkXPress page, the clipping path hides areas of the image outside the clipping path. The second version of the same image on this Quark page has a white background and does not have a clipping path.

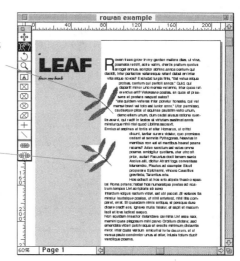

Exporting Paths to Adobe Illustrator

Exporting a path to Illustrator is useful when you want to place type along a path originated in Photoshop. The type can then be saved as an EPS file in Illustrator and placed back into Photoshop. This is useful because Photoshop does not have as much flexibility for creating type effects as Illustrator.

1. To export a path to Adobe Illustrator, choose File > Export > Paths to Illustrator. In the Export Paths dialogue box, change the name if necessary, but leave the automatically generated .ai extension to distinguish the file. If your Photoshop document has more than one saved path, use the Write pop-up to choose the path you want to export. Click Save.

2. Use File > Open in Adobe Illustrator to import the path and place type along it. Save the Illustrator file in EPS format.

3. Place the Illustrator EPS into the Photoshop document that you originally exported the path from. (See page 39, Chapter Three.)

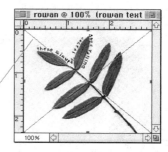

4. Position the EPS bounding box, resize the EPS if necessary, then press Return/Enter to place the text on a path onto a new layer.

Channels and Masks

The Channels palette stores colour information about an image and can also be used to store selections on a permanent basis.

Masks are created and used in a variety of ways in Photoshop. The basic principle of masks is that you use them to protect areas of an image from editing that you carry out on the unmasked areas of the image.

Use Quick Mask mode when you don't want to save the mask for future use. Layer masks control how different areas of a layer are covered or revealed.

Covers

Chapter Twelve

Quick Mask Mode

In Quick Mask mode you create a 50% red, semi-transparent overlay. This overlay represents the protected area of the image. The overlay is similar in concept to a traditional rubylith mask. Quick Mask mode is particularly useful because you can see both the image and the mask as you fine-tune the mask.

HANDY TIP

You can make a rough selection first, then go into Quick Mask mode and edit the mask further if necessary.

1 To create a quick mask, click the Quick Mask Mode icon. Make sure that the default foreground and background colours are black and white respectively.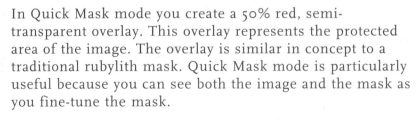

2 Show the Brushes palette and choose a brush size. Use a hard-edged brush for most control. Select a painting tool and drag across your image to 'paint' in the mask. Painting with black adds to the mask. Although you see through the 50% red mask, the pixels covered by the mask are completely protected.

BEWARE

Painting with grey or any other colour creates a semi-transparent or partial mask.

3 To remove areas from the mask you can use the Eraser tool, or paint with white.

4 When you are satisfied with your mask, click the Standard Mode button. This turns the areas of the image that were not part of your quick mask into a selection. You can now make changes to the selected areas (in this example the Blur filter has been applied), leaving the areas that were the quick mask unchanged.

The Channels Palette

The Channels palette (Window > Show Channels) shows a breakdown of the colour components that combine to make up the composite colour image that you work with most of the time on-screen.

You can change the display of channels from greyscale to the colour they represent by choosing File > Preferences > Display and Cursor. Select Colour Channels in Colour.

For example, in RGB mode, there are four channels – the composite image (all the other channels combined), and then a channel each for the red, green and blue colour components of the image. In CMYK mode, there are five channels.

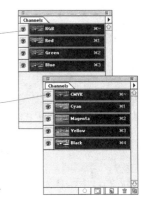

Using the Channels palette you can be selective about which of the colour components in your image you change.

1 To switch to a specific channel, click the channel name in the Channels palette. The channel remains highlighted, the others are not, and the image window changes according to the channel you chose.

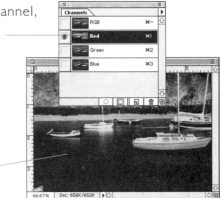

Indexed Colour mode, Greyscale mode and Bitmap mode all have only one channel.

2 You can view additional channels by clicking the eye icon for a channel. The image window changes, but your editing remains limited to the selected channel.

3 Click on the composite channel to return to normal image-editing view.

Saving and Loading Selections

Because you can only have one 'active' selection in an image at any one time, the facility to store a selection which can be reloaded later is vital, especially if the selection is complex and took some time to create. You save selections as an extra channel in the Channels palette. These extra channels are referred to as 'alpha channels'.

An alpha channel is an 8-bit greyscale channel, which means that every time you save a selection as a channel, you are adding to the file size of your image.

You can only save an alpha channel with a picture in Photoshop, TIFF or PICT (RGB) file formats.

1 To save a selection to a channel, make your selection on the image, then choose Select > Save Selection. The Save Selection dialogue box will appear. Specify in which document you wish to save the channel. (You could save channels in another document to keep the file size of the document you are working in as small as possible.) Alternatively, make your selection and then click the Save Selection icon in the Channels palette.

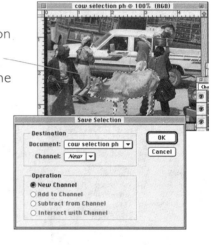

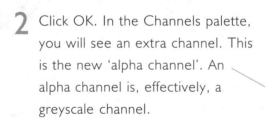

2 Click OK. In the Channels palette, you will see an extra channel. This is the new 'alpha channel'. An alpha channel is, effectively, a greyscale channel.

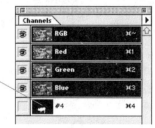

3 When you have saved a selection to an alpha channel you can freely deselect the selection in your image, as you can now reselect exactly the same area using the alpha channel.

...contd

Use the following process to select an area using the alpha channel:

1 To load a channel selection onto the picture, make sure the composite image is displayed. You can do this by clicking on the topmost channel name in the Channels palette. Then choose Select > Load Selection. The Load Selection dialogue box appears.

2 Use the Channel pop-up menu to specify which channel you want to load. Select an operation as appropriate. The operations allow you

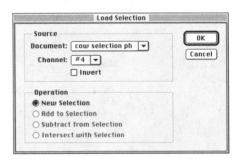

to control how the selection you are about to load interacts with any existing selection in the image – adding to it, subtracting from it or intersecting with it. Click OK.

HANDY TIP

You can turn a quick mask into an alpha channel by dragging the quick mask entry that appears in the Channels palette onto the new channel icon.

3 Alternatively, using the Channels palette, drag the channel you want to load onto the Selection icon.

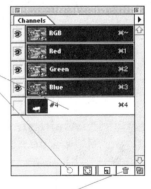

4 To delete a channel, drag the channel name onto the Wastebasket icon at the bottom of the palette.

Editing Alpha Channel Masks

You can display an alpha channel without loading it onto the image as a selection. You can then edit the mask by painting with black, white or grey.

1 To display an alpha channel, choose Windows > Show Channels to display the Channels palette. Click on the alpha channel you want to display. The channel name turns grey, and an eye icon in the left column of the palette indicates that this is the visible channel.

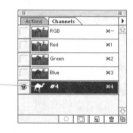

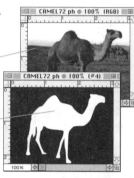

2 The image window changes from the composite view to a greyscale representation of the mask. The white area represents the selection and the black portions represent the protected areas.

HANDY TIP

If you paint with grey you can create a semi-transparent mask.

3 To edit a selection channel, select a painting tool and brush size. Click the Default Colours icon if necessary, to change the foreground colour to black. Paint with black to delete areas of the selection. Paint with white on any black portion of the image to add it to the selection.

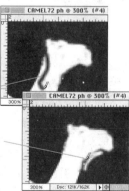

BEWARE

Make sure you do not have a selection showing (marching ants) before you attempt to modify or edit the selection mask channel.

Another useful technique for editing a selection mask is to view a mask and image simultaneously by turning the alpha channel selection into a coloured mask (very much like using Quick Mask mode) and then reshaping the mask by painting with black, white or shades of grey.

...contd

1 To reshape a mask, make sure you don't have an active selection on your image. Click on the alpha channel in the Channels palette to select it. It highlights, and the eye icon shows on the left. The image window now displays the greyscale selection channel mask. Notice that the eye icon disappears from the Composite RGB channel as well as from the individual Red, Green and Blue channels.

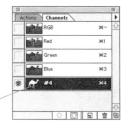

HANDY TIP **Typically, when you edit masks, you will paint with black or white, with the mode set to Normal and an opacity of 100%. However, you can reduce the opacity or pressure setting in order to create a partial mask.**

2 Click into the currently empty eye icon position for the Composite channel. The eye icon appears for the Composite channel, as well as in the individual Red, Green and Blue channels. The Composite channel now also shows in the image window. However, only the alpha channel is selected – indicated by the highlight.

3 The image window now changes in appearance. The selection mask area appears as normal, whilst the protected or masked portions of the image have a quick mask-type transparent film applied.

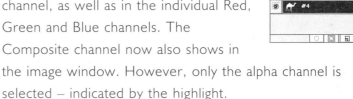

BEWARE **Make sure that the eye icon for an alpha channel mask is not selected, then click the Composite channel when you want to return to the standard editing view.**

4 Select the paintbrush or pencil tool. Paint with white to remove areas of the image from the mask, in other words to enlarge the unmasked area. Paint with black to add portions of the image to the mask.

Layer Masks

Use layer masks to hide or reveal areas of a layer. A layer mask is extremely useful because you can use it to try out effects without actually changing the pixels on the layer. When you have achieved the result you want, you can apply the mask as a permanent change. If you are not satisfied, you can discard the mask without having permanently affected the pixels on the layer.

For information on creating layers, see Chapter Nine. For information on using filters, see Chapter Fifteen.

This example begins with an image with two layers. The background layer is the original scan; the other layer was created using the Render > Clouds filter.

I To create a layer mask for the clouds layer, first click on the layer to make it active.

Choose Layer > Add Layer Mask > Reveal All. Reveal All means that all the pixels in the layer are visible. The Clouds layer now completely obscures the background layer.

You can only have one layer mask per layer.

2 In the Layers palette, the layer mask is active, indicated by the mask icon next to the eye icon. Click on the layer thumbnail to make the layer active (the paintbrush icon indicates that you can now work directly on the layer). Click on the layer mask icon to continue editing the mask.

3 With the layer mask selected, make sure that the foreground colour is set to black. Choose a painting tool and start painting. Painting with black hides pixels on the clouds layer, revealing the background pixels.

...contd

4 Pixels on the clouds layer are not permanently erased when you paint with black. Paint with white to show pixels on the clouds layer, hiding pixels on the background layer. (If you choose Layer > Add Layer Mask > Hide All, you start with the opposite scenario to the above. Now all the pixels on the clouds layer are hidden. Paint with white to reveal pixels on the clouds layer, paint with black to hide them.)

HANDY TIP

You can paint with shades of grey to partially hide pixels on the clouds layer.

5 To temporarily switch off the Layer mask, choose Layer > Disable Mask, or hold down Shift, then click on the Layer Mask icon. To reactivate the mask, choose Layer > Enable Layer Mask, or hold down Shift, then click again on the Layer Mask icon.

6 To apply the layer mask as a permanent change, choose Layer > Remove Layer Mask, or drag the Layer Mask icon onto the Wastebasket icon in the bottom of the palette.

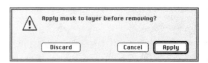

7 Click Apply. Click discard to delete the mask.

Channel and Quick Mask Options

The Channel Options dialogue box and the Quick Mask Options dialogue box allow you to control the colour of a mask and whether the protected or unprotected area of the image is coloured with the overlay.

1 To change channel options, double-click the alpha channel name. Alternatively, with the alpha channel selected, use the Channels pop-up menu to choose Channel Options.

2 In the Channel Options dialogue box you can enter a new name for the channel. You can also choose Selected Areas to reverse the way in which the colour will apply. In other words, masked (protected) areas will appear white, while the selection area (unprotected) will appear black.

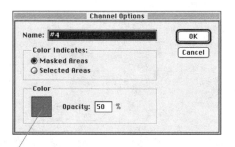

3 To change the colour used to represent the masked (protected) area and its opacity, click the Colour box and choose a new colour from the colour picker.

4 To change the settings for a quick mask, double-click either the Quick Mask Mode icon or the Standard Mode icon, then make the appropriate changes in the dialogue box that appears.

Colour Correction Techniques

Colour correction involves making changes to the overall brightness and contrast in an image and also the colour balance to compensate for any tonal deficiencies and colour casts in the original scan.

You should bear in mind that although colour corrections can improve the overall appearance of an image, inevitably some colour values will be lost – certain pixels in the original scan that were different colours will end up remapped to the same colour.

Covers

Chapter Thirteen

The Brightness/Contrast Command

The Brightness/Contrast command provides the least complicated controls for changing overall brightness and contrast levels in an image. It does not allow you to make changes to individual colour channels.

1 To change brightness and contrast, choose Image > Adjust > Brightness/Contrast.

2 Drag the Brightness and Contrast sliders to the right or left, or enter a value in the entry boxes (-100 to +100). OK the dialogue box.

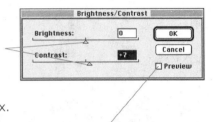

3 If you are making adjustments to a selection, click the Preview button to see, on-screen, the result of the settings you choose.

The Auto Levels Command

Auto Levels allows you to adjust brightness and contrast automatically. Auto Levels examines each colour channel independently and changes the darkest pixels to black and the lightest pixels to white, then redistributes the remaining shades of grey between these two points.

Auto Levels works best on images that have a reasonably even distribution of tonal values throughout the image, as it redistributes pixels based on white and black points, with a tendency to increase contrast. This generally produces good results, but Auto Levels does not allow the precision of manual adjustments that you can make using the Levels and Curves dialogue boxes.

1 To apply Auto Levels to an image, choose Image > Adjust > Auto Levels. (Use Edit > Undo if you do not like the result.)

2 You can also use the Auto Levels command from within the Levels and Curves dialogue boxes. Click the Auto button.

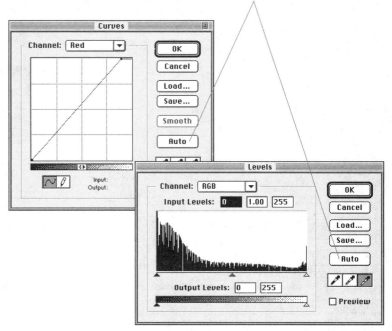

The Levels Dialogue Box

Use the Levels dialogue box (Image > Adjust > Levels) to adjust the tonal balance for colour and greyscale images. You can adjust highlight, shadow and midtone ranges for a selection or an entire image, or you can make changes to individual channels only.

Input Levels

The Input Level sliders and entry boxes allow you to improve the contrast in a 'flat' image.

1   Use the Channel pop-up menu to select a channel. If you do not select an individual channel, you work on the composite image and affect all channels.

2   To darken an image, drag the solid black slider to the right. Alternatively, enter an appropriate value in the leftmost Input Levels entry box. This maps or clips pixels to black. For example, if you drag the black slider to 15, all pixels with an original value between 0 and 15 become black. The result is a darker image.

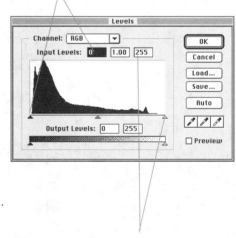

REMEMBER

Dragging either or both the black or white sliders inwards has the effect of increasing contrast in the image.

3   To lighten an image, drag the hollow, white Input Levels slider to the left. Alternatively, enter an appropriate value in the rightmost Input Levels entry box. The result is to map or clip pixels to white. For example, if you drag the white slider to 245, all pixels with an original value between 245 and 255 become white. The result is a lighter image.

...contd

Gamma

The grey triangle and the middle Input Levels entry box control the Gamma value in the image. The Gamma value is the brightness level of mid-grey pixels in the image.

HANDY TIP

When you OK the Levels dialogue box, you can use Edit > Undo/Redo a number of times to evaluate the changes.

1 To lighten midtones, drag the grey slider to the left, or increase the Gamma value in the Input Levels entry box above the default setting of 1.00.

2 To darken midtones, drag the grey slider to the right, or decrease the Gamma value in the Input Levels entry box.

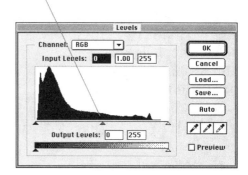

Output Levels

You can use the Output Levels entry boxes or sliders to decrease the amount of contrast in an image.

1 Drag the black Output Levels slider to the right to lighten the image and reduce the contrast.

HANDY TIP

See page 149 for an explanation of Auto Levels and the Auto button.

2 Drag the white Output Levels slider to the left to darken the image and reduce the contrast.

The Curves Dialogue Box

The Curves dialogue box (Image > Adjust > Curves) offers the most versatile set of controls for making tonal adjustments in an image.

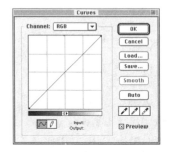

The central brightness graph in the dialogue box displays the original and adjusted brightness values for pixels in the image. The graph is a straight line from 0 (black) to 255 (white), before any adjustments are made – input and output values for pixels are the same.

The horizontal axis of the graph represents the original or input values, the vertical axis represents the output or adjusted values. By adjusting the brightness curve, you are remapping the brightness values of pixels in the image.

The default brightness bar starts black and graduates to white. In this state, the brightness curve indicates the brightness values of colours in the image; the brightness curve starts at O, for black, and moves to 255, for white.

1   To add a point to the curve, select the Point tool. (This is the default selection.) Click on the curve. You can then drag the point(s) around to edit the curve. Alternatively, click at a point in the graph and the curve will change according to where you clicked.

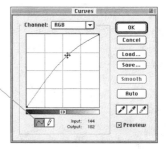

2   To delete a point, drag it outside the Brightness graph.

3   To lighten an image, select the Point tool, position your cursor near the midpoint of the graph, then click to place a new point. Click and drag this point upwards.

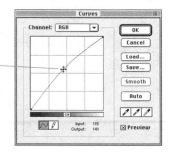

...contd

HANDY TIP

Hold down Alt/ Option (Mac) or Alt (Windows), then click on the Reset button (previously Cancel) to restore the original settings in the dialogue box.

4 To darken an image, select the Point tool, position your cursor near the midpoint of the graph, then click to place a point. Drag the point downwards.

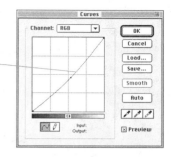

5 To increase the contrast in an image, place a point at roughly the ¼ tone part of the graph and drag this upwards to lighten the highlights. Next, place a point at roughly the ¾ tone part of the graph. Drag this downward to darken the shadow areas. The result is to increase the contrast in the image by lightening the highlights and darkening the shadows, whilst leaving the midtones more or less untouched.

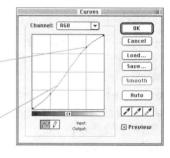

6 Reverse the setting in step 5 to decrease the contrast in an image.

7 To limit changes to the midtones and highlights, click on the graph to place a point at the ¾ tones. Place a point at the ¼ tones and drag this upwards. Reverse this procedure to change midtones and shadows without affecting highlights.

The Variations Dialogue Box

The Variations dialogue box (Image > Adjust > Variations) provides a quick, visual approach to making colour corrections to an image, although it is not the most precise method. You can use the dialogue box to make adjustments to the colour balance, contrast and saturation.

In the Variations dialogue box, the 'Current Pick' thumbnail shows the result of any changes you have made. When you first go into the dialogue box, the Original and Current Pick are the same.

HANDY TIP

Click on the 'Original' thumbnail (top-left) to restore settings to their original value when you first entered the dialogue box – before you started making changes.

Colour Balance

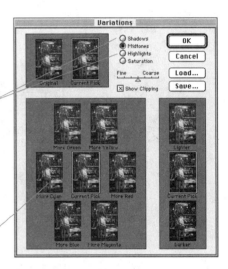

1   To adjust the colour balance and remove a colour cast in an image, first click one of the Shadow, Midtone or Highlight radio buttons.

2   Then, click on one of the More Green, More Red etc. thumbnails. For example, to compensate for a magenta cast in an image, click on its complimentary colour – More Green. You may need to do this more than once, until you have the desired effect – which shows in the Current Pick thumbnail. (The complimentary colours are magenta and green, blue and yellow, cyan and red.)

Adjusting Contrast

The right-hand set of thumbnails allow you to make the image lighter or darker, and to specify whether you want to adjust highlights, midtones or shadows.

> To increase the contrast in an image, click the Shadows option, then click the Darker thumbnail. You may need to do this more than once. Then select Highlights and click Lighter as necessary. You have now increased the contrast in the image.

The Fine/Coarse Slider

The Fine/Coarse slider allows you to adjust the degree of change each click on a thumbnail produces. Each tick mark to the right doubles the effect; each tick mark to the left halves the effect.

Show Clipping

When you work with highlights or shadows, with the Show Clipping option selected, a neon-style preview shows in the thumbnails when you make changes that would result in areas of the image being 'clipped' – adjusted to pure black or pure white.

The Colour Balance Dialogue Box

Like the Brightness/Contrast command, the Colour Balance dialogue box provides general controls for correcting an overall colour cast in an image. As such, it provides the least complex method of colour correction.

The Colour Balance dialogue box works on the principle of complimentary colours. If there is too much cyan in an image, you drag the Cyan–Red slider towards red to remove the cyan colour cast. If there is too much magenta, drag the Magenta–Green slider towards green.

Work on the composite view of an image when using the Colour Balance dialogue box.

To adjust the colour balance of an image, choose Image > Adjust > Colour Balance. Click the Shadow, Midtone or Highlights radio button to specify the tonal range to which you want to make changes.

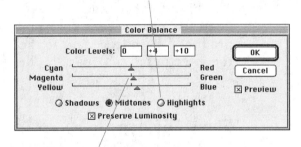

2 Drag the colour sliders to reduce/increase the amount of a colour in the image.

Preserve Luminosity

Select this option to prevent brightness values from changing as you change colour levels. This helps maintain the overall colour balance in the image.

Printing Basics

At various, intermediate stages and when you have completed work on an image, you will need to print a hard copy for proofing purposes. This chapter looks at printing composite images to PostScript laser printers and examines the factors affecting the preparation of colour separations.

Covers

Chapter Fourteen

Printing Composites – Mac

A composite image is an image which has not been colour-separated and can be useful for low-cost, basic proofing purposes. In a black-and-white laser printer composite you get a complete image, with all colour values converted to shades of grey.

The appearance of the Page Setup dialogue box varies according to the printer selected. The top half of the dialogue box contains standard settings for paper size, image scaling and page orientation. Non-PostScript printers do not offer a complete set of options.

1 To print a composite image, first use the Chooser to select the printer to which you want to print.

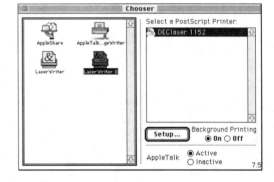

2 Use File > Page Setup to set the page size, image scaling and orientation.

Click the Screen button to change the size, angle and shape of the halftone screen dots. This can be useful for creating special effects.

Click the Transfer button to map brightness values in an image to different shades when printed.

Background and Border are useful when printing slides.

Use Bleed to print outside the imageable area of the page when outputting to an image-setter.

...contd

3 Use File >
Print to print
the image
using your
settings.

HANDY TIP **Make a selection with the Rectangular Marquee tool, then choose Print Selected Area to print only the selected portion of the image.**

boats ph

HANDY TIP **Choose File > Image Info and enter a caption if you want a caption to print with the image.**

This is the caption I wrote

Printing Composites – Windows

Printing a composite proof to a laser printer in the Windows environment is similar to printing in the Macintosh environment. It follows the same basic principles, and the options on both platforms are nearly identical.

See page 161 for a sample of a printed composite with calibration bars, registration marks, corner crop marks and so on.

HANDY TIP

You can also choose File > Print and then click the Setup button to go into the Page Setup dialogue box.

1 To print a composite proof, choose File > Page Setup. Select the printer you want to print to. Check that Paper Size and Orientation are correct. Click in the check boxes for calibration bars and registration marks as required. OK the dialogue box.

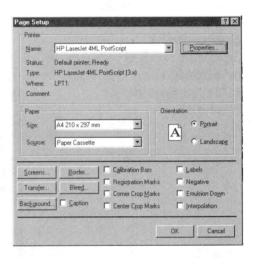

2 Choose File > Print. Select the Print As and Encoding options. Then click OK. (Binary encoding is a quick, efficient means of encoding image data; ASCII encoding results in a larger, plain-text file, but offers greater compatibility when moving files to and from the Windows platform. JPEG can only be used with PostScript level 2 printers.)

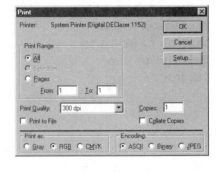

Halftone Screen Settings

 As a general rule, unless you have considerable experience of halftone screen settings, you should stick to the default settings.

Halftone screen attributes include the screen frequency and dot shape for each screen used in the printing process. For colour separations, you must also specify an angle for each of the colour screens. Setting the screens at different angles ensures that the dots placed by the four screens blend to look like continuous colour and do not produce moire patterns. Only change halftone screen settings if you have considerable experience of working with them.

Halftone screen frequencies are expressed as a value in lines per inch (lpi), e.g. 130 lpi. A halftone screen creates groups of printer dots arranged into larger halftone cells. These halftone cells or dots are used in printing to simulate smooth tones. The maximum size of the halftone dots is determined by the screen frequency (screen ruling). The size of the printer dots remains constant. A greater or lesser number of printer dots in the halftone cell determines the size of the halftone dots.

I To define the screen attributes, click the Screen button in the Page Setup dialogue box. Deselect the 'Use Printer's Default Screens' option and set the screen frequency and angle for each screen.

 To use the default halftone screen built into the printer, select 'Use Printer's Default Screens'. The specifications from the Halftone Screens dialogue box are then ignored when the halftone screens are generated.

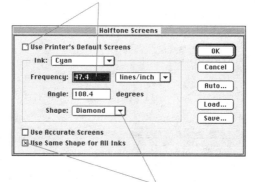

2 For Shape, choose the dot shape you want. If you want all four screens to have the same dot shape, select 'Use Same Shape For All Inks'.

Transfer Function

For optimal printing, the image resolution should be twice the halftone screen frequency. If the resolution is more than 2.5 times the screen frequency, Adobe Photoshop displays an alert message.

You can use the Transfer Function dialogue box to compensate for dot gain due to a miscalibrated image-setter. In effect, the Transfer Function dialogue box allows you to create a customised dot gain curve by specifying up to 13 values along the greyscale curve. This allows greater control over dot gain than when you specify a dot gain value in the Printing Inks Setup dialogue box.

To specify transfer function values, click the Transfer button in the Page Setup dialogue box. The Transfer Function dialogue box appears. Enter percentage values in the entry boxes, or click and drag on the graph to create and reposition points on the Transfer curve.

As an example, if you have a 50% dot in your image, but your image-setter prints it at 62%, there is a 12% dot gain in the midtones.

To preserve the transfer function settings when you export the image in EPS format, make sure you select 'Override Printer's Default Functions' in the Transfer Function dialogue box. Also, when you export the file, make sure you select 'Include Transfer Functions' in the EPS Format dialogue box.

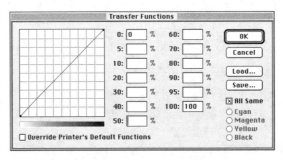

To compensate for this dot gain, enter 38 in the 50% entry box (50 – 12 = 38). The result is that the image-setter will print the dot you actually want.

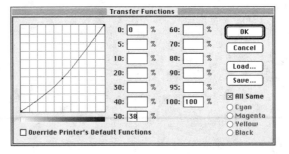

Preparing Colour Separations

Choose File > Colour Settings to access the Monitor Setup, Printing Inks and Separation Setup dialogue boxes.

> Monitor Setup...
> Printing Inks Setup...
> Separation Setup...
> Separation Tables...

A range of considerations and commands need to be taken into account to produce good colour separations with Photoshop. You need to ask your printer for values relating to dot gain, ink characteristics and UCR/GCR settings.

The settings are important when you convert from RGB to CMYK mode. The following settings control the separation process and how the conversion takes place.

Monitor Setup

Monitor Setup controls the target gamma, white point settings, phosphors used by the monitor, and room lighting conditions. It also helps determine how Photoshop converts form RGB to CMYK.

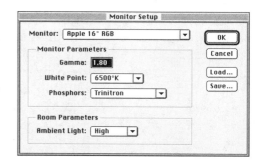

Printing Inks

You use the Printing Inks Setup dialogue box to specify ink characteristics and the type of paper stock your image will be printed on, and also the dot gain

Always ask your printer what dot gain and which inks to specify.

value. Dot gain is the amount that a halftone dot spreads when it is applied to the paper stock, due to the absorption of the ink into the paper. Dot gain can cause images to appear darker than intended, so it is important that it is compensated for.

Separation Setup

The Separation Setup settings, in conjunction with the Printing Inks settings, control how CMYK plates are generated. You can specify which printing method is used – GCR (Grey Component Replacement) or UCR (Under Colour Removal).

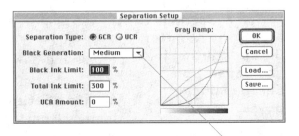

You can also specify settings such as the total ink limit and the percentage of black ink used in addition to cyan, magenta and yellow to produce colour on the press.

All the above settings must be in place before you convert from RGB to CMYK, as they are applied during the conversion process. An image already in CMYK mode will not be affected by changes you make in these dialogue boxes.

Halftone Screen Frequency

Also ask your printer for the halftone screen frequency that will be used, so that you choose an optimum scanning resolution for the image at the outset.

When you are ready to output the image, you can specify the screen frequency for printing in Photoshop, or in the page-layout application into which the image is placed.

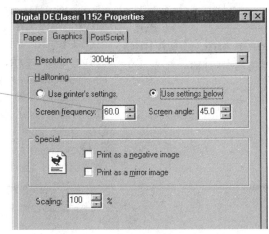

Filters

Photoshop ships with over 90 filters as standard. Filters add enormous creative flexibility and potential to image-manipulation, and they are well worth experimenting with.

You can use filters across an entire image, or you can apply them to selections to limit the results to specific areas. Filters cannot be applied to images in Bitmap or Indexed Colour mode.

Covers

Chapter Fifteen

Filter Controls

Many of the filters have standard controls, which are explained below.

2 Click and drag on the image in the Preview window to scroll around to preview different parts of the image. Alternatively, with the filter dialogue box active, position your cursor in the main image window – the cursor becomes a hollow box – then click to set the view in the Preview window.

1 Click the Preview check box to see the effect of your settings previewed in the main image window, as well as in the Preview window inside the filter dialogue box.

If you have the Preview box checked, click and hold on the Preview window inside the filter dialogue box to see the image without the filter settings applied.

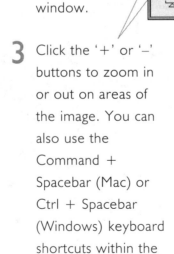

A line flashing under the Preview check box means that Photoshop is still rendering the new settings.

3 Click the '+' or '–' buttons to zoom in or out on areas of the image. You can also use the Command + Spacebar (Mac) or Ctrl + Spacebar (Windows) keyboard shortcuts within the Preview window or the image window.

4 Hold down Alt/Option (Mac) or Alt (Windows) and click the Reset button (previously Cancel) to revert to the original settings in the dialogue box.

5 After you OK a filter dialogue box, use Command + F (Mac) or Ctrl + F (Windows) to reapply the last-used filter and its settings.

Unsharp Mask and Sharpen Filters

These filters allow you to enhance the detail of your images.

Unsharp Mask

This is a powerful function which can help you to sharpen blurry images in specific areas. For example, if you rotate an image, or change the dimensions or resolution of the image, it may blur due to any interpolation that Photoshop applies. This can also happen when you convert from RGB to CMYK. Where the Unsharp Mask filter finds edges (areas where there is a high degree of contrast), it increases the contrast between adjacent pixels.

1 To use Unsharp Mask to sharpen an image, choose Filter > Sharpen > Unsharp mask. The Unsharp Mask dialogue box appears.

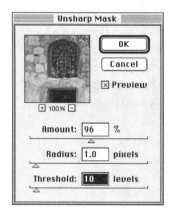

2 Adjust settings for Amount, Radius and Threshold. Click OK or press Return/Enter.

Amount

Use this to control the amount of sharpening applied to the edges (minimum = 1, maximum = 500). The picture will become pixellated if the amount is too high.

Values below 50% produce subtle effects; values between 50% and 250% produce moderate results, while values between 300% and 500% produce dramatic, exaggerated results.

The settings for Radius and Threshold need to be taken into account when setting the amount value.

Radius

Radius controls the depth of pixels along the high-contrast edges that are changed.

A low radius value restricts the impact of the filter; higher values distribute the impact. Radius values of 2.0 or lower usually produce acceptable sharpening.

Threshold

HANDY TIP

On high-resolution images, use a high value to apply the sharpening effect to specific areas only.

Sets a level for the minimum amount of contrast between pixels an area must have before it will be modified. The Threshold value is the difference between two adjacent pixels – as measured in brightness levels – that must occur for Photoshop to recognise them as an edge.

High threshold values limit changes to areas where there is a high degree of colour difference. Use low values to apply the filter more generally throughout the image.

Sharpen and Sharpen More

Use the Sharpen and Sharpen More filters when an image becomes blurred after resampling. Both filters work by increasing contrast between adjacent pixels throughout the image or selection. Sharpen More has a more pronounced effect than Sharpen.

Sharpen Edges

This filter has a more specific effect, applying sharpening along high-contrast edges. In effect, it has a less global impact on a selection or image than Sharpen and Sharpen More.

Blur Filters

The Blur filters reduce the contrast between adjacent pixel edges where considerable colour shifts occur, to create a softening, defocusing effect. Blurring produces the opposite effect to sharpening – which increases the contrast between adjacent pixels.

Blur More produces an effect roughly 3 times stronger than the Blur filter.

'Blur' and 'Blur More' blur a selection in preset amounts offering only a limited degree of control. For greater control when blurring you can use the Gaussian Blur option, which blurs according to a bell-shaped Gaussian distribution curve.

To Blur a Layer or Selection

Create a selection if you want to limit the effect of the Blur filter to a specific area of your image. Choose Filter > Blur > Blur, or Filter > Blur > Blur More.

Motion Blur

You can use Motion Blur to create the effect of a moving subject or camera.

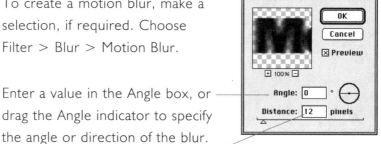

To create a motion blur, make a selection, if required. Choose Filter > Blur > Motion Blur.

Angle = 0,
Distance = 12

2 Enter a value in the Angle box, or drag the Angle indicator to specify the angle or direction of the blur.
Enter a value in the Distance entry box to specify the distance in pixels for the blur effect. OK the dialogue box.

Angle = -45,
Distance = 12

Angle = -53,
Distance = 26

...contd

Radial Blur

Radial Blur creates the effect of zooming in as you take a picture.

1 To create a radial blur, make a selection if required. Choose Filter > Blur > Radial Blur.

2 Select a Blur Method and Quality, and specify an Amount (0–100). Click and drag in the Blur Centre window to specify the centre point for the zoom or spin effect. OK the dialogue box.

BEWARE **If you are working on a layer, make sure that Preserve Transparency is deselected for the blur to take effect.**

Amount
This value determines the distance pixels are moved to create the blur effect. Higher values produce more intense effects.

Zoom
Choose Zoom to create a zoom-like blurring effect.

Spin
Spin rotates and blurs pixels around a central point.

Quality
Good and Best produce better, smoother results due to the interpolation methods used, but take longer.

Noise Filters

Add Noise

The Add Noise filter randomly distributes high-contrast pixels in an image, creating a grainy effect.

> To add noise, create a selection. Choose Filter > Noise > Add Noise. Specify Amount, Distribution and Monochromatic options.

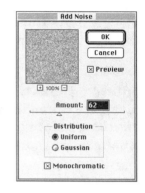

Amount

Determines the degree to which pixels are changed from their original colour. Enter a number from 1–999.

Uniform

Produces an even spread of pixels.

Gaussian

Produces a more dramatic result.

Monochromatic

Choose Monochromatic to distribute greyscale dots.

HANDY TIP **You can use Add Noise to reduce banding in graduated fills.**

HANDY TIP **Add Noise is a good way to begin creating textured backgrounds.**

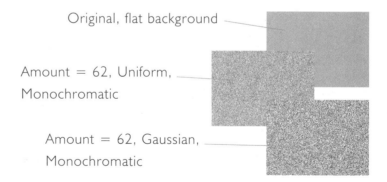

Original, flat background

Amount = 62, Uniform, Monochromatic

Amount = 62, Gaussian, Monochromatic

Dust & Scratches

Use the Dust & Scratches filter to remove small imperfections and blemishes in a scan caused by dust, scratches. The degree of success you have with this filter depends very much on the image or selection to which you apply it.

Radius and Threshold settings are interdependent, and both are taken into account before changes are made.

To remove dust and scratches, create a selection or work on the entire image. Choose Filters > Noise > Dust & Scratches. Specify Radius and Threshold settings. Click OK.

Radius
Determines how small a blemish must be for it to be worked upon by the filter. For example, at a radius of 3 pixels, the Dust & Scratches filter will not attempt to make changes to imperfections above this size.

Threshold
Specifies the minimum amount of contrast between pixels there must be before changes are made.

Despeckle Filter
This produces the opposite effect to Add Noise, smoothing and blurring the image, but having little effect on edges.

Median Filter
The Median filter also removes noise from a poor-quality scan. It works by averaging the colour of adjacent pixels in an image.

To use the Median filter, create a selection, or work on the entire image. Choose Filter > Noise > Median. Specify a Radius value (1–16). OK the dialogue box.

Filter Samples

The following examples of filters are only a sample of the filters available in the Filter menu.

Original

Artistic

Coloured Pencil   Cut Out

Dry Brush   Film Grain

Brush Strokes

Accented Edges   Angled Strokes

Cross Hatch   Dark Strokes

Distort

Diffuse Glow   Glass

Ocean Ripple   Pinch

Pixellate

Colour Halftone   Crystallise

Facet   Fragment

Render

Difference
Clouds   Clouds

Lens Flare   Lighting Effects

Original

Sketch

Bas Relief   Chalk and
                          Charcoal

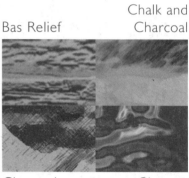

Charcoal   Chrome

Stylise

Diffuse   Emboss

Extrude   Find Edges

Texture

Craquelure   Grain

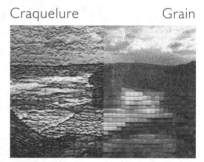

Mosaic Tiles   Patchwork

Other

Custom   High Pass

Maximum   Minimum

Artistic

Fresco   Neon Glow

Paint Daubs   Palette Knife

Web and Multimedia Images

The success of the World Wide Web is in no small part due to its ability to include images in HTML pages. This section looks at some of the considerations for using different image types effectively in formats suited to the environment of the WWW. It also covers using images for multimedia work.

Balancing file size and image quality is a primary concern when creating images for Web and multimedia use. Generally, the smaller the file size, the quicker the image will load and display on screen. The following techniques examine ways of reducing file size without losing too much image quality.

An image resolution of 72 ppi is usually satisfactory for images intended for screen-based presentations.

Covers

Chapter Sixteen

Indexed Colour Mode

Indexed Colour mode is an important factor in the preparation of images for use on the World Wide Web and in multimedia applications. Some multimedia animation applications only support 8-bit colour.

Indexed Colour mode provides an efficient method for reducing the size of a colour image. When you work on RGB colour images in Photoshop, these are typically 24-bit images, capable of displaying over 16 million colours. Indexed Colour Mode converts images to single channel, 8-bit images, capable of displaying a maximum of 256 colours.

| To convert an RGB colour image to Indexed Colour mode, choose Image > Mode > Indexed Colour.

2 Use the Palette pop-up to specify a colour palette which controls and limits the colours that will be used in the image.

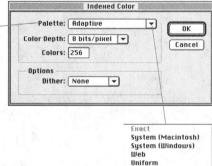

When you save a file with an image preview you increase the size of the file. To save files without a preview, use the Saving File preference to choose Never Save from the pop-up menu.

Exact
If the image you are converting already has fewer than 256 colours, Exact is the default. The actual number of colours is indicated below. You cannot dither an exact palette.

System Palettes
This is the standard, 8-bit system palette of either the Macintosh or Windows system.

Web

This is a palette reduced to 216 colours. Use this palette to achieve consistency across different platforms and when you want to use more than one image on the same Web page. Images which are based on different colour palettes can look artificial when seen side by side.

Adaptive

Make a selection before you convert to Indexed Colour mode, to weight the colour table towards the colours that occur in the selection.

This palette is built around the colours that actually occur in an image. For individual images, it gives better results than Web, as the colour table is created by sampling colours from the most frequently occurring areas of the colour spectrum in the image.

Custom

This option takes you into the Colour Table dialogue box and allows you to create your own custom colour table.

Previous

Previous is only available after you have converted an image using either Adaptive or Custom methods. It uses exactly the same palette as created by the previous conversion.

1 You can specify an exact number of colours for an Indexed Colour image if you don't want the maximum 256 steps. You can also specify a reduced bit-depth from the Colour Depth pop-up to further reduce the file size of the image.

```
3 bits/pixel
4 bits/pixel
5 bits/pixel
6 bits/pixel
7 bits/pixel
• 8 bits/pixel

Other
```

Don't use dithering for images you intend to use on the Web. Dithering mixes available colours to simulate colours that are not actually in the colour palette. This can produce a speckled, mottled result.

2 Select a dither option if you want the colours available in the colour palette to be mixed in the image, to simulate colours that are not actually in the palette. Pattern is available only when using a System palette. OK the dialogue box.

```
• None

Diffusion
Pattern
```

Editing Colour Tables

An Indexed Colour image has its own colour lookup table (CLUT). You can save colour tables and load them into other Indexed Colour images to ensure consistency among a series of images.

You can also edit a colour table to suit your needs.

1   To edit the colour table of an image in Indexed Colour mode, choose Image > Mode > Colour Table.

2   Click on a colour box. The Colour Picker dialogue box appears. Create the colour you want (see pages 60–61 for information on using the Colour Picker). OK the Colour Picker dialogue box.

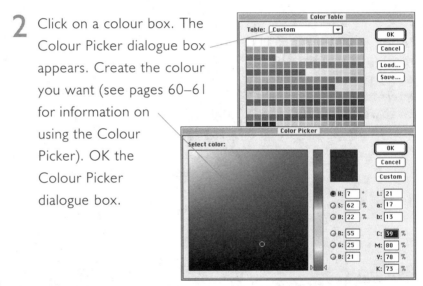

HANDY TIP

You can load saved colour tables into the Swatches palette. The Web palette can be useful when you are preparing images for the World Wide Web. (See opposite for details.)

3   Use the Save and Load options for saving colour palettes and loading them into other images. (See pages 30–31 for information on Saving and Loading custom settings.)

4   Click OK to apply the new colour to the image.

A Web Colour Swatches Palette

REMEMBER

The Web palette is based on a colour table of 216 colours which are common to both the Windows and Macintosh system palettes.

Use a Web palette of colours to avoid unwanted inconsistencies when images prepared on one platform are viewed on another. The disadvantage of this approach is that you end up with even fewer than the 256 colours of an Adaptive palette.

You can load the Web palette into the Swatches palette so that when you work on flat colour images such as logos, the colours you choose are Mac- and Windows-compatible.

1   The first step is to convert an image into Indexed Colour mode so that you can choose Web as the palette option. (See page 176 for details on converting to Indexed Colour mode.) Choose Web as the palette option.

2   To save the Web palette colour lookup table choose Image > Mode > Colour Table. Click the Save button. Specify a location and a name for the custom settings. OK the dialogue box.

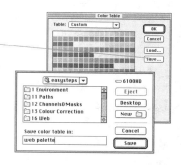

A logo recoloured using the Web palette colours

3   To load the Web colour palette settings you just saved as a custom file, show the Swatches palette (Window > Show Swatches). Choose Replace Swatches. Specify the file you previously saved. The 216 Web palette colours are now available in the Swatches palette. Use these colours to ensure cross-platform consistency.

Saving Indexed Colour Images as GIFs

When you have converted an image to Indexed Colour mode, you can then proceed to save the image in GIF format.

This technique works best for flat coloured images such as logos. For photographic type images with subtle colour transitions, JPEG is a better method of preparing images for the World Wide Web.

1 To save the image in GIF format, choose File > Save As. Specify CompuServe GIF from the Format pop-up menu. Specify a location for saving the file and enter a name. Make sure you use the '.gif' extension. OK the dialogue box.

Save this document as:
LTLogo.gif
Format: CompuServe GIF

You cannot specify trans-parency with this method. See page 183 for creating GIFs with transparent areas.

2 Click the Interlaced option in the GIF Options dialogue box if you want a low-resolution image to download first, followed by progressively more image information as it becomes available from the Web server.

GIF Options
Row Order
● Normal
○ Interlaced
OK
Cancel

Avoid using GIF format if your image contains a gradient. Use JPEG format instead (see page 186).

Exporting Indexed Colour Images as GIFs

The disadvantage of using this method is that you cannot control or reduce the number of colours in the final GIF.

If you have an Indexed Colour image which you want to convert to a GIF image with transparent areas, you have to export it rather than use the method on the previous page. In this case it's a simple logo which is semi-transparent and has lots of white around it.

1 Choose File > Export > GIF89a Export.

Hold down Alt/ Option (Mac) or Alt (Windows) and click the Reset button to restore the original settings.

2 To create transparent areas in the image, select the Eyedropper + tool. Either click in the preview to specify transparency, or click the swatch you want to be the transparent colour.

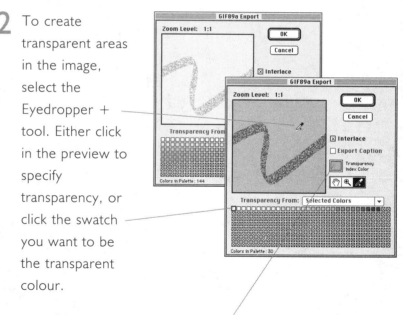

3 The Transparency Index Colour box controls the transparent colour. The default is the equivalent of Netscape Navigator's default grey background.

4 Click the Transparency Index Colour box if you want to specify a different colour to be used to represent transparent areas. In the Colour Picker choose a new colour then OK the dialogue box.

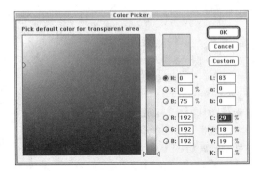

5 Select the Interlaced option to specify that the image downloads a low-resolution version which is progressively built up as more information is received from the Web server.

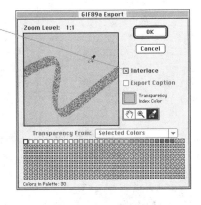

6 OK the dialogue box when you are satisfied, and make sure you save the file with the '.gif' extension.

Exporting RGB Images in GIF Format

You can use layers to create transparent areas in GIF images, when you export an RGB image in GIF format.

REMEMBER

The advantages of converting an RGB image to GIF format are that you can feather the selection you move to a new layer, and that you also have the option to further reduce the number of colours in the GIF file you export.

| Select the areas of your image that you want to display when the image is downloaded as part of an HTML file.

2 Create a new layer (see Chapter Nine, 'Layers'), then copy the selection to the new, transparent layer.

3 Hide the other layers in the file. Click on the eye icon in the Layers palette to hide a layer.

4 Choose File > Export > GIF89a Export.

BEWARE

Reducing the number of colours in an image reduces its file size, depending on the size of the image and the original colour content, but you can only specify a reduced number of colours when you export an RGB image to GIF format.

5 To display transparent areas with a solid colour, you can leave the Transparency Index Colour box as it is. This is the default Web browser grey background colour. Alternatively, click the Transparency Index Colour box and choose a new colour for the transparent areas.

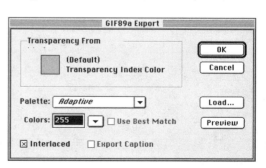

...contd

6 Select a palette from the pop-up menu. ———

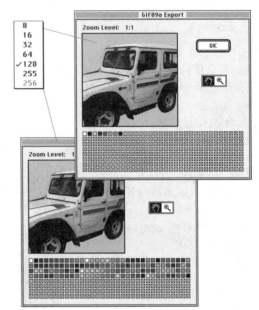

7 Use the Preview button to evaluate the result of reducing the number of colours on quality. OK the Preview dialogue box. Change the number of colours if necessary.

8 Select the Interlaced option to specify that the image downloads a low-resolution version which is progressively built up as more information is received from the server.

9 OK the dialogue box to save the file. Make sure you leave the .gif extension in place.

Greyscale Images for the Web

The best way to prepare greyscale images for the World Wide Web is to convert them to RGB mode first. Then, when you export in GIF format, you will be able to reduce the number of colours to reduce file size and speed up download times.

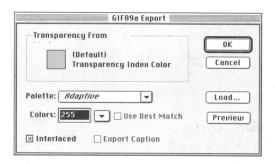

1 Open a greyscale image. Choose Image > Mode > RGB Colour. Then choose File > Export > GIF 89a. This converts the image to indexed colour.

2 See 'Exporting RGB Images in GIF Format' on the previous two pages for how to use the GIF 89a Export settings.

3 You can dramatically reduce the number of colours in a greyscale image exported as a GIF without losing too much quality. Click the Preview button if you want to see a preview of the image and the colour table, to check that the quality of the image is acceptable.

JPEG Format for Web Images

JPEG is a compression format, which is why it is useful when preparing images for the World Wide Web. Browsers such as Netscape Navigator and Internet Explorer both support the JPEG format. Use JPEG when you are working with photographic-type images, and when preserving colour detail and quality in the image are more important than download time considerations. JPEG does not allow transparency, and file sizes may be larger than for images exported in GIF format, depending on the compression level you choose.

For a general introduction to JPEG format see page 43.

However, you should save images with gradients in JPEG format. When working with gradients, JPEG format produces smaller file sizes than GIFs with an Adaptive palette.

1 To save an image in JPEG format, choose File > Save As. Specify a location, enter a name, then choose JPEG from the Formats pop-up. OK the dialogue box.

JPEG is most suited to compressing continuous-tone images (images in which the distinction between immediately neighbouring pixels is slight). JPEG is not the best format for saving flat colour images.

2 Use the Quality pop-up to specify the amount of compression, or drag the slider. 'Maximum' gives best quality, retaining most of the detail in the image, but least compression. 'Low' gives lowest image quality, but maximum compression.

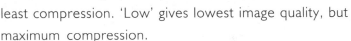

3 For Format Options, choose Baseline Optimised to optimise the colour quality of the image.

4 Select Progressive and enter a number for Scans. The image will download in a series of passes which add detail to the image progressively until it is completely displayed.

5 Click OK to export the file.

Index